Single-Parent Families

SAGE SOURCEBOOKS FOR THE HUMAN SERVICES SERIES

Series Editors: ARMAND LAUFFER and CHARLES GARVIN

Recent Volumes in This Series

HEALTH PROMOTION AT THE COMMUNITY LEVEL
edited by NEIL BRACHT

**TREATING THE CHEMICALLY DEPENDENT
AND THEIR FAMILIES**
edited by DENNIS C. DALEY & MIRIAM S. RASKIN

HEALTH, ILLNESS, AND DISABILITY IN LATER LIFE:
Practice Issues and Interventions
edited by ROSALIE F. YOUNG & ELIZABETH A. OLSON

ELDER CARE: Family Training and Support
by AMANDA SMITH BARUSCH

FEMINIST SOCIAL WORK PRACTICE IN CLINICAL SETTINGS
edited by MARY BRICKER-JENKINS, NANCY R. HOOYMAN,
& NAOMI GOTTLIEB

SOCIAL WORK PRACTICE WITH ASIAN AMERICANS
edited by SHARLENE MAEDA FURUTO, RENUKA BISWAS,
DOUGLAS K.CHUNG, KENJI MURASE, & FARIYAL ROSS-SHERIFF

FAMILY POLICIES AND FAMILY WELL-BEING:
The Role of Political Culture
by SHIRLEY L. ZIMMERMAN

FAMILY THERAPY WITH THE ELDERLY
by ELIZABETH R. NEIDHARDT & JO ANN ALLEN

EFFECTIVELY MANAGING HUMAN SERVICE ORGANIZATIONS
by RALPH BRODY

SINGLE-PARENT FAMILIES
by KRIS KISSMAN & JO ANN ALLEN

Single-Parent Families

Kris Kissman
Jo Ann Allen

Sage Sourcebooks for
the Human Services Series
24

SAGE Publications
International Educational and Professional Publisher
Newbury Park   London   New Delhi

To Shawn, Thor, and Tammy

For information address:

SAGE Publications, Inc.
2455 Teller Road
Newbury Park, California 91320

SAGE Publications Ltd.
6 Bonhill Street
London EC2A 4PU
United Kingdom

SAGE Publications India Pvt. Ltd.
M-32 Market
Greater Kailash I
New Delhi 110 048 India

Printed in the United States of America

Library of Congress Cataloging-in-Publication Data

Kissman, Kris
  Single-parent families / Kris Kissman, Jo Ann Allen.
      p.   cm. —(Sage sourcebooks for the human services series ;
  24)
  Includes bibliographical references and index.
  ISBN 0-8039-4322-9 (cl). —ISBN 0-8039-4323-7 (pb)
  1. Family social work—United States. 2. Single-parent family—
United States. I. Allen, Jo Ann. II. Title. III. Series: Sage
sourcebooks for the human services series : v. 24.
HV699.K58   1993
362.82'94'0973—dc20   92-35502

93 94 95 96   10 9 8 7 6 5 4 3 2 1

Sage Production Editor: Tara S. Mead

CONTENTS

PREFACE

Practitioners working with families are increasingly being sensitized to issues related to diverse family structures, particularly the one-parent family. But the family-centered practice literature still does not devote a great deal of space to assessment and intervention with one-parent families, who now constitute more than one-fourth of all families. Because one-parent families do not constitute a homogeneous group, our aim in this volume is to delineate treatment issues that are based on such factors as the gender of the head of household, ethnicity, age, and sexual orientation. Much of our attention is devoted to interventions with mother-headed families; these women and children often face economic hardships, and the mothers are subject to negative societal expectations about their ability to head families. We emphasize the important roles of social policies and services that help mothers meet the challenging dual roles of caregivers and wage earners.

In our practice with these families we have found that interventions based on gender-sensitive principles, combined with other family-centered strategies, help to accentuate the strengths these families possess. These interventions focus on mobilizing supportive networks and encouraging mothers to name their experiences rather than to attribute family problems to personal inadequacies. Family-centered interventions such as ecomapping take on special meaning for single mothers, to whom strong support networks are often essential for respite child care and economic survival. Similarly, family stories can help deconstruct those experiences that placed the family in the pejorative category of "nonintact" families. We share the view of many practitioners that societal perceptions of one-parent families, and especially mother-headed families, constitute a powerful factor that works against these families.

The organization of this book is based on the view that the single-parent family is one of many family forms and is characterized by a great deal of within-group variation. Single parents as a heterogeneous group comprise an increasing number of individuals who have chosen to parent alone and who have never married. The majority of single parents, however, are divorced, separated, or widowed, and for this group the realignment of the family system following separation is a primary concern. Interventions range from help in restructuring the division of labor within the family to creating a participatory form of decision making and a greater reliance on external support.

Although we stress the significance of lack of resources in social work intervention with single parents, it should be noted that half of all single-parent families live above the poverty line. Maternal age differences account for great variations in the well-being of these families. Adolescent parents are more vulnerable to economic impoverishment than are older mothers, and comprehensive services that help a young mother stay in school are critical to the welfare of mother and child. Teen mothers, compared with their older counterparts, often have greater need for training and education in parenting skills, child development, and utilization of a support network.

Variations in single-parent families also stem from family life cycles. Reliance on extended family and extrafamilial support systems for respite child care is a critical factor when children are young, while coping with adolescent individuation is a later life-cycle task that is especially challenging for mothers who attribute developmental changes to inadequate family structure.

Race and ethnicity both have impact on the practitioner-family relationship. Ethnicity-sensitive practice requires the worker's self-awareness about his or her own ethnicity and feelings about cultural diversity. Practitioners should also have an understanding of how ethclass (the combination of ethnicity and class) has generated survival strengths, such as flexible system of exchange and community and family collectivity, among many ethnic families.

Changing gender roles and shared parental responsibilities have led to increased attention being paid to the role of the noncustodial parent in strengthening single-parent families. Treatment issues center on how to parent at a distance and how to negotiate a more active parental role for the absentee parent, who may be able to assume coparental responsibilities.

As increasing numbers of custody decisions award joint or sole custody to fathers, single fathers as heads of families sometimes need help in assuming a more central role in their children's lives. This socialization process often entails diffusion of parent-child boundaries; some fathers need to learn to attend to and nurture their children as well as provide for their material needs.

A cross-national comparison of the economic and social positions of mother-headed families reveals that a much larger proportion of these families are impoverished in the United States than are those in countries such as Scandinavia and that the negative view of the single-parent family also varies across cultures. These comparisons help legitimate the view, held by many feminist practitioners, that the disempowered status of the mother-headed family is not inevitable. They also indicate that comprehensive family policies, such as vigorous child support enforcement and affordable child care, are sorely needed if mothers are to combine child rearing and wage labor successfully.

We wish to thank our many colleagues at the University of Michigan School of Social Work who have read chapters of the manuscript and who have made helpful suggestions. We are particularly grateful to our colleague and series editor, Charles Garvin, who gave us intermittent feedback along the way and guided us throughout this endeavor. We also wish to thank the many authors who have contributed their thoughts toward our efforts.

Chapter 1

GENDER-SENSITIVE PRACTICE WITH SINGLE-PARENT FAMILIES

The feminist influence in social work is reflected in the publication of several books and articles on the topic in the past few years. A large part of this literature is aimed at revising traditional theories and practice to reflect the needs of women clients more closely and to promote gender-sensitive assessment of problems associated with women as caregivers and wage earners. A feminist practitioner enables clients to determine the extent to which their problems are the result of sexist practices and stereotypes (Whittaker & Tracy, 1989).

Some of these works have been published by the National Association of Social Workers, which also conducted a national study identifying some of the strengths of single-parent families. The development of feminist social work parallels the contribution of feminist family therapists, who have published extensively on the topic in the past several years (Kissman, 1991). These two sources of knowledge development are influencing therapeutic practice with women, many of whom are single heads of households.

Feminist practice is not a series of skills and techniques applicable to therapeutic intervention with women, with single heads of households, or with families and individuals in general, but a practice based on major principles derived from feminist thought. These principles are being applied in the development of perspectives that can be used to revise existing knowledge and theories guiding interventions. These revisions are

1

deemed essential by feminist theorists and practitioners, who have criticized traditional interventions with women as often gender biased and hurtful to women's welfare in general. The application of feminist thought in therapeutic practice is not limited to work with women, but extends to work with families, individuals, and groups.

Feminist-based practice goes by many names, including woman-centered practice (Hanmer, Stratham, & Sancier, 1989), nonsexist practice (Burden & Gottlieb, 1987), and feminist practice (Bricker-Jenkins & Hooyman, 1986; Collins, 1986). Feminist-based practice with families is referred to as feminist family therapy (Avis, 1988; Walters, 1988).

The term *gender-sensitive practice* is used throughout this book to describe intervention with men and women and *feminist-based practice* is used to emphasize the special needs of women clients. These terms reflect a developing and revisionary, rather than new, practice perspective with individuals, male and female. This perspective is politically based and aims at ending domination and oppression through the empowerment of individuals who have traditionally found themselves on the bottom rung of power hierarchies. Empowerment is a process through which clients obtain resources, including personal resources, that enable them to attain their aspirations and gain control over their environments (Hasenveld, 1987).

Because most single-parent families (nearly 90%) are headed by women (U.S. Bureau of the Census, 1989a), and because mother-headed families are particularly vulnerable to negative evaluation and economic hardships, we focus primarily on ways to strengthen these families. We have chosen to address the special problems facing the increasing proportion of single-parent families headed by fathers in a separate chapter.

The issues addressed in this chapter include the identification of some of the feminist premises that guide gender-sensitive practice and the application of these premises to practice with mother-headed families. We begin with an assessment of how negative biases and mother blaming infringe on the welfare of single-parent families. Next, we discuss and exemplify interventions aimed at legitimating the role of mothers as heads of families. A case example provides illustration of how a mother's role as an executive head of the family often needs to be affirmed as a first step in strengthening the system. Positive connotations about the capacity of these families to meet challenges associated with life-cycle changes need to be articulated before extended family members and partners are marshaled for support, not rescue.

Next, we turn our attention to the promotion of participatory pattern of interaction within the family and in professional relationships. The participatory decision-making style that is often the norm in mother-headed families requires that practitioner-family interactions also be based on gender-sensitive egalitarian premises. And a joint problem-solving effort between worker and client is a requisite model for interventions aimed at creating participatory family dynamics. Further elaboration of how family dynamics interconnect with a larger environment begins with the worker-family relationship and continues toward a holistic view of policies, programs, and services as integral components of family interventions. Family economic welfare is particularly germane in our interventions with impoverished families, but family diversity is based on such factors as economic resources, gender of the head of household, ethnicity, age, and family life-cycle stage.

NEGATIVE VIEWS OF SINGLE-PARENT FAMILIES

The negative attitude on the part of society toward mother-headed families works against these families in their attempts to provide support functions for family members (McLanahan, 1983). The dual roles that single mothers perform provide challenges that are better met with optimism and a "can do" attitude than with internalized negative expectations. Societal disapproval concerning single-mother families stems from a lack of faith in women's capacity for executive leadership. Women have often been considered as the "other" of mankind, and the mother-headed family suffers similar categorization as the "other" of family systems (Sands & Muccio, 1989).

Consciousness-raising about the impact of such gender biases on the welfare of families and reframing of negative expectations are lavishly used by gender-sensitive practitioners as intervention strategies. Studies emphasizing a pessimistic view of single parents and equating such families with crime and delinquency are being disputed by feminist family theorists and practitioners (e.g., Lupenitz, 1988). Family structure has been blamed for the impact of poverty, racial discrimination, and other social ills.

Research evidence indicates that the majority of single-mother families are as successful as two-parent families when compared on measures of emotional adjustment and scholastic achievement (Cashion,

1982). Adolescent parents, as subgroups of single-parent systems, have special difficulties related to their own developmental needs and lack of economic resources. While some children from single-mother families suffer lower self-esteem than those from two-parent homes, this can be attributed to prejudiced social opinions and negative expectations rather than family structure (Cashion, 1982).

Since 27% of all families are now headed by single parents (U.S. Bureau of the Census, 1989b), such families can hardly be termed *anomalous*. Current studies deemphasize the polarized view of families as being "functional" or "dysfunctional" based primarily on family structure. The shift away from pathology and negative labeling of the "broken" and "nonintact" home toward a problem-solving framework helps to identify the needs that are relevant to carrying out the goals of the family.

Clearly, problem assessments and interventions are influenced by practitioners' views as to what constitute normative and viable family systems. Whether a practitioner views the executive single-parent system as "functioning independently" or as "incomplete" is closely related to problem assessment, intervention, and outcome.

Negative expectations about the capacity of mothers to parent alone extend to therapeutic relationships as well. Observations of persistent mother blaming in traditional therapeutic encounters exemplify problems associated with the low status of women in general and the attribution of their powerlessness within family systems (Caplan & Hall-McCorquodale, 1985). Indeed, family therapy may be dangerous to women's mental health, as articulated by Goldner (1985). Mother blaming has been so prevalent that, in a review of major clinical journals, Caplan and Hall-McCorquodale (1985) found no fewer than 72 different psychological disorders attributed to mothers' failings. This negative perspective is amplified in cases in which mothers head families. Such views ignore the historical base of family systems. During wars and in many cultures, single parenting has been a norm and a functional type of system (Figueira-McDonough & Sarri, 1987).

INTERVENTIONS
TO STRENGTHEN FAMILIES

In a recent survey of social workers, practitioners reported that feminist practice is characterized by networking, empowerment, and emphasis on women's experiences (Bricker-Jenkins & Hooyman, 1986). The first two of these concepts are applicable to the practice of social work in general, but the unique status of women in the context of society and within family systems calls for special emphasis on the ways these principles are applied to practice with women.

Practitioners can help to empower the mother-headed family by counteracting the negative stereotype of women as ineffective in carrying out the executive functions of the family. As suggested by Levy Simon (1990), clients empower themselves with the help of practitioners who can provide the climate, a relationship, resources, and procedural means for empowerment. The gender-sensitive practitioner legitimates the role of the mother as single parent by stressing that, contrary to popular opinion, mother-headed families can be competent and successful in nurturing, socializing, and supporting children. Normalization is often best accomplished in self-help groups for single mothers, where experiences related to negative stereotypes of the mother-headed family are shared and successful strategies for responding to these encounters can be established.

Well-meaning friends and acquaintances, for example, often make unfavorable comments indicating that the single-parent family is not a capable system and is even to be pitied. Many single parents can respond effectively by sharing that the choice to parent alone was made because it is less problematic than the two-parent system, which was fraught with conflict and perhaps even violence. In cases in which the parent has never married, responses indicating the prevalence and success of many single parents can prove effective in stifling comments reflecting negative stereotyping. One woman recalled that she felt empowered when she offered to reciprocate the help her new neighbors had extended to her as a single parent obviously in need of help.

The practitioner's ability to affirm the role of single parents as normative and potentially functional is contingent upon the extent to which he or she has integrated feminist-based principles into practice. The gender-sensitive practitioner has a realistic view of changing gender roles in today's society and recognizes that the notion of the single-parent family as inadequate to meet the needs of its members is gender biased and leads to an impasse in working with these families. Because so many mother-headed families remain one parented, practitioners must explore alternatives for strengthening these families as intact units.

The positive aspects of single parenting are emphasized in the National Association of Social Workers study reported by Shore (1986).

Single mothers in this study cited lack of conflict in child-rearing decisions, family harmony, strong support networks of family and friends, and increased independence for parent and child as some of the strengths of their families. Although single-parent families need not be perceived of as preferred structures, the concept of diverse family forms reflects the reality of today's families.

Practitioners who seek ways to aid in the empowerment of the mother-headed family begin with how they join the family and continue to transmit their belief about mothers' competence and self-efficacy throughout the process of intervention. The strength of these systems can be harnessed in various ways, ranging from the realignment of the internal structure to greater utilization of supportive networks.

The techniques used in feminist-based practice are similar to those used in conventional interventions, but reframing the problem as the mother's lack of confidence in her new role, rather than her inability to head the family successfully, often differentiates the two types of interventions. Reinforcement and positive connotation to enhance the mother's competence in her role as head of household are often used more lavishly in gender-sensitive practice, as is affirmation of the legitimate status of single-parent families in general.

Walters (1988) cites the following case example, which illustrates how a feminist therapist used empowerment strategies to strengthen the support network and the internal structure of a mother-headed family. A custodial mother of two sons, ages 17 and 15, sought family therapy to resolve conflicts regarding her older son's school attendance, non-compliant behavior at home, and alcohol use. The mother felt inadequate about raising her male children alone and frustrated because the absentee father provided negligible assistance. The therapist intervened by articulating positive connotations regarding the mother's capacity to raise her children as a single parent.

The second component of the intervention was to work on conflicts in the potentially supportive relationships with the boys' grandmothers. This "network therapy" consisted of helping the mother develop empathy for and identify similarities in the lives of the women in the extended family. All the women in the family had lived with alcoholic spouses, and the identification of trends in the family history served to create a common bond and closer relationships among the women in the family. Support from the maternal and paternal grandmothers included the latter's encouraging her son to play a greater part in caring for his children.

The third phase of the intervention was focused on setting and maintaining enforceable, age-appropriate rules and on encouraging shared decision making in matters affecting the quality of life of this one-parent household. After the mother's capacity to head the household had been affirmed and the supportive network and internal structure were strengthened, the support of the absentee father was mobilized. The children's father was encouraged to pay regular visits, while the mother worked on maintaining a distant but workable relationship with him. At this point, the mother had moved from the role of victim toward planning future career goals, continuing her education, and resuming dating.

This case is a good example of a starting point of any feminist-based therapy, that of moving from a perception of the mother-headed household as a deficit model toward strengthening the focal point of the structure, the executive system. Because negative stereotypes have often minimized the ability of mother-headed families to function effectively, they often must be strengthened from within before they can be connected to both extended and extrafamilial networks. Mother and children can greatly benefit from strong support networks that buffer problems associated with enmeshment, disengagement, scapegoating, and other boundary difficulties between the executive and sibling subsystems. The need for support should not be viewed as reflective of women's inadequacy to head families.

Mother blaming may become particularly intensified during that part of the family life cycle when adolescent individuation and separation needs compound to devaluate the mother's status within the family. In Walters's example, a dominant male "parental" child attempted to take charge, consistent with his socialization into a dominant male role.

PROMOTING A
PARTICIPATORY VERSUS HIERARCHICAL
PATTERN OF FAMILY INTERACTION

In the above case illustration, gender-sensitive practice can be said to reorder the priorities of intervention. The problem for work becomes partialized as a part of the process of mother empowerment, followed by the mobilization of support and other related issues. Conventional intervention would tend to make a priority issue of securing the help of the absentee father, thereby reinforcing the family's own insecurity regarding the competence of the mother as an executive head.

It is true that father support is often a critical factor related to the general well-being of the mother-headed family. Fathers who continue to be involved with their children following divorce or separation can provide needed emotional, financial, and task support, all of which make an important difference in the overall adjustment of the family. Ahron and Rodgers (1987) suggest that when we refer to the single-parent family as *binuclear* rather than *single*, we normalize the involvement of the absentee father in the lives of his children. Shared parental responsibility in single-parent families may increase as we come to view the binuclear family as one of many diverse family forms.

In reality, the frequency of noninvolvement by absentee fathers in the lives of their children suggests that if mother-headed families are to be strengthened they must be viewed as whole systems. Yet, families without fathers often have difficulty seeing themselves or convincing others that they are complete systems. This is especially true in light of paternal authority and the traditional role of father as provider of family resources.

Traditional family therapy is based on hierarchical authority, with father as executive head in the two-parent family. Conversely, gender-sensitive practice emphasizes participatory rather than hierarchical structure of family interactions. A participatory perspective deemphasizes rather than eliminates power and authority from above. This deflation of power hierarchies is not synonymous with disengaged or chaotic family interaction patterns. Particularly during the last phases of the family life cycle, the mother moves to an advisory role, with the children taking on increased responsibility for tasks and decision making. Children in one-parent families grow up to assume a great deal of responsibility, which often proves to be positive for their own growth and development (Amato, 1987).

In contrast to the use-it-or-lose-it power premise of hierarchical family patterns of interaction, feminist thinking views power as not limited but infinite, so that empowering some individuals does not necessarily imply that others must lose power. Feminist-based emphasis on a more vertical power hierarchy still relies on traditional theories, including family systems and the ecological perspective, as explanatory models for family interactions.

The unique characteristics of the interface between the mother-headed family and the environment, however, require that a special gender-sensitive focus be applied. The one-parent family, for example, tends to rely heavily on the "parental" child, who may act as a parent's confidante and perform functions that interfere with the child's own development (Morawetz & Walker, 1984). The danger of enmeshment and dysfunctional cross-generational alliances in the one-parent family may not be dissimilar, however, to the dynamics in two-parent structures in which the father is on the periphery and does not assume the responsibilities associated with the executive role.

EGALITARIAN PROFESSIONAL RELATIONSHIPS

The feminist principle that advocates equality of status, roles, tasks, and decision making within families extends to therapeutic relationships as well. Hierarchical as opposed to vertical distribution of power in any interpersonal interaction inevitably contradicts the feminist-based premise of individual empowerment. In client-centered therapy, the practitioner does not claim to have ultimate power to diagnose, but strives toward joint assessment and goal formulation.

Although joint assessment is an integral part of the social work contract, gender-sensitive practice is more than just "good" social work practice. The gender-sensitive practitioner has confronted his or her own values regarding traditional gender roles and views the problems confronting single-parent families as closely related to the status of women in society rather than based on individual deficit.

The gender-sensitive practitioner prioritizes the empowerment of the single parent, who may suffer from the "worried well syndrome," or feeling that parenting alone is necessarily fraught with faults (Goodrich, Rampage, Ellman, & Halstead, 1988). Mothers who parent alone often have internalized the negative views of society concerning single parenting, and they tend mistakenly to attribute problems associated with adolescent individuation and other developmental phases of the family life cycle to inadequacies in the one-parent family structure. Power equalization between worker and client in social work is clearly related to empowerment that derives from naming one's experiences and assessing personal problems within a contextual frame, such as the effects of discrimination and lack of resources on one's life.

A HOLISTIC VIEW OF THE FAMILY

Among the feminist premises identified by Van Den Bergh and Cooper (1986) as specifically relevant to social work practice are (a) that the personal is political, and (b) that the right to name one's own experience is critical for self-understanding and identity. A holistic view of families acknowledges multiple factors that create "functional" family units. The structure of the family does not in itself determine how well family members are able to cope. Economic factors, levels of support, and other "contextual" factors are as important as level of competence and other individual attributes.

Gender-sensitive practice is based on a multidimensional view of families within a broader context of society. This view emphasizes the interconnection between the individual and political experiences of women and their status within the family and society as a whole. Understanding of the contextual aspects of individual interaction with the environment is enhanced by an examination of how the individual problems of women as single heads of households are tied to women's status within society.

The ecological perspective helps the practitioner assess the multiple "living" systems that orbit a client in crisis and how this interaction affects the problem for work. Feminist practice expands this framework to include how gender influences individual interaction with the environment. Lack of economic resources often creates conditions whereby many impoverished mother-headed families reach crisis level in their daily lives when one of the children becomes ill or when transportation breaks down and family livelihood is at risk.

The gender-sensitive practitioner understands that the negative societal view of the single-parent family is attributable to devaluation of individuals based on gender and that the results are a wide gender gap in earning and low wages among women. The depressed economic condition of mother-headed as opposed to father-headed households indicates that gender is a powerful predictor of poverty.

Adolescent births do lower the earning power of women by limiting the capacity for career preparation. Women who bear children at age 27 or older earn 37% higher incomes than do women who become parents by the age of 20 (Bloom, 1987). However, women's educational levels now parallel those of men and do not account for the high incidence of poverty among women. Nor does time devoted to child-rearing responsibilities explain lower wages among women, since male heads of households earn 50% higher wages than single mothers who work full-time (U.S. Bureau of the Census, 1985).

Lack of child support payments paid by fathers in this country promotes poverty among single mothers and their children. Only one-third of single mothers receive child support, and two-thirds of the payments are less than the court ordered (Goodrich, Rampage, & Ellman, 1989). In contrast, 90% of Scandinavian single mothers receive full child support payments (Gunnarsdottir & Broddason, 1984). Child support payments can be more aggressively pursued, as can mothers allowance benefits, which have been initiated in 117 countries, but not in the United States (Hewlett, 1986).

Although practitioners have limited influence and power to create more equitable distribution of resources within society at large, the gender-sensitive practitioner is an advocate of policy changes that affect the welfare of women and children. Lack of compensatory mothers allowance, child support enforcement, and affordable day care become part of problem identification in work with single-parent families.

The recognition of how gender biases adversely affect the welfare of women must be coupled with an understanding of racial biases that further serve to depress the economic status of women and children. Women and children of color are much more likely to be living in poverty than are their white counterparts. Nearly 40% of children in white single-parent families are poor, while nearly 67% of children in African-American and Hispanic mother-headed families live below the poverty line (Danziger, 1989).

The feminist-based emphasis on the right of women to name their own experiences is particularly relevant to impoverished mothers who are both caregivers and wage earners. Employment, in itself, does not reduce poverty among this group of women and children. Single mothers must earn at least $6 per hour and have adequate child-care and health services to raise their families out of poverty (Bane, Ellwood, Jargowsky, & Wilson, 1989). Our empathy toward children living in poverty must extend to the reality of mothers' poverty and the fact that when basic needs go unmet, every aspect of the "therapeutic" encounter is related to this lack of resources. We cannot prescribe recreational activities, for example, to counter stress-related symptoms for mothers who lack the resources for respite child care and transportation.

The gender-sensitive practitioner identifies the multiple needs of women wage earners and caregivers and serves as a mediator and a broker in helping clients secure needed resources to carry out these dual roles. Practitioners must perform the difficult task of helping to bridge the gaps in services created by policies that do not reflect the important connection between the wage earner and caregiver roles of women. Workfare programs requiring women receiving public assistance benefits to seek paid employment, for example, initially ignored the fact that most of the new and available jobs being created pay minimum wage, and lack health care and affordable child-care benefits. The linear thinking that equates employment with the reduction of poverty among women and children needs to be replaced with a more multifaceted view of supportive services and/or adequate wages to pay for such services.

It is true that many of the issues that have negative impacts on the welfare of single mothers also affect working mothers in general: Child-care problems and role overload are common among mothers in those two-parent homes where there is little sharing of parental responsibilities. And not all single-parent families are poor or in need of assistance, but poverty, whether of time or of money, is a distinguishing characteristic of many custodial mothers who perform multiple roles.

Chapter 2

TRANSITIONAL STAGES
AND THE FAMILY LIFE CYCLE

Even though increased numbers of single parents have never married and have chosen to parent alone, many experience a difficult transitional phase following divorce, separation, or widowhood. Interventions are often aimed at helping the family respond to economic changes, realignment of the family structure, and support utilization, especially following divorce or separation. Economic changes, for example, have great impact on family well-being, because most single-parent families are headed by women, and their incomes are much lower than those of their male counterparts who parent alone. While 50% of mother-headed families live below the poverty line, only 8% of father-headed single-parent families are poor (Pearce, 1990). Added responsibilities of day-to-day activities tend to be compounded by severe economic decline following divorce or separation. These families need to mourn reduced income and lowered standard of living, which may include loss of home, neighborhood, friends, and status of the two-parent family.

Family members initially tend to respond to changes in the family structure with a lowered sense of competence. Lack of competence on the part of members of one-parent families is often caused by reduced resources, by negative societal messages about the inadequacy of the single-parent household, and by increased demands on time, skills, and energy. The practitioner can communicate positive connotations about positive aspects of the restructured family system. Emphasis must be placed on the family's strengths and its capacity to function as a whole and intact unit. Bringing in a father or male partner as a rescuer is likely to affirm the family's transitional difficulties, whereas helping the custodial parent to assert her right to share coparenting responsibilities with an absentee parent can facilitate the healing process.

Families who continue to respond to the old structure or who operate in a holding pattern, waiting to be relieved from the temporary status of single parenting, are likely to experience difficulties in coping with the often overwhelming demands of the new structure. Realignment of the new system requires a gradual acceptance by family members of its new form. After the often difficult initial postdivorce period, however, many women have found renewed strength and confidence in their ability to work and to care for their families alone. Various studies have found that despite economic disaster, women after divorce often significantly improve the quality of their lives (Wallerstein, 1986).

In this chapter we discuss interventions aimed at facilitating realignment and adjustment by family members to the new family form. Late life-cycle stage needs, for example, tend to be associated with changes in the division of labor among family members. Following divorce or separation, custodial parents may need to give up some conventional expectations regarding housekeeping tasks and functions in order to provide increased support, nurturance, and socialization to autonomous and responsible family members. In the interest of family cohesion, tidy surroundings should receive a lower priority, in terms of time expenditure, than should supportive interactions about daily activities. Reestablishing family rituals, including regularly scheduled family sessions, family-practitioner contract negotiations, normalization of the adolescent period, and time management are additional strategies used to facilitate collaborative and cohesive single-parent family structures.

Many families experience multiple transitions simultaneously when new partners become part of the family shortly after the initial parental separation. The effect of divorce on the children is greatly contingent on the relationship between the mother and father, and this relationship becomes more complex when sequential stages of transition do not take place, but instead separation and then reconstitution of the family occur simultaneously or within a very short period of time. Although the parameters of single parenting do not apply to other diverse family forms, such as remarried families, we do include interventions aimed at strengthening support from partners in our discussion of support from partners in Chapter 5.

FUNCTIONAL REALIGNMENT
OF THE INTERNAL STRUCTURE

Among the primary changes encountered by the single-parent family are the period immediately following divorce and separation, adjustment to the parental role when the children are young, and the process of adolescent individuation. Factors such as level of support, economic resources, and skills in restructuring daily interactions account for some of the great variations with which family members successfully respond to and realign the one-parent structure. The practitioner helps the family during the early stages of the family life cycle to develop and utilize external support systems to the fullest extent. Chapter 8 expands on the early life-cycle phase when children are young and the single mother's adjustment to the parental role is highly contingent on extended family and extrafamilial support systems.

Later life-cycle issues center on adolescent individuation. This period can be problematic in any family type, but it can be extremely painful in the one-parent family where parental separation and then parent-child separation occur almost simultaneously. Parental role and authority are shifted to one parent, particularly when the absentee parent is not involved with child-rearing responsibilities. Empathy training and family rituals that promote positive, nurturing patterns of interaction can help make the transition less traumatic, as can interventions aimed at developing contracts between mother and child to resolve conflicts over decisions and responsibilities. Issues of acceptance/rejection are manifested in power struggles over who does what, when, and how. Conflict resolutions are inextricably linked to division of labor in the home and management of time. The family restructures itself in the process of decision making about task performance and curfews and, ideally, by way of a participatory decision-making pattern in which members are free to develop some autonomy. We will provide an example of how contract agreements can help resolve some of the struggles between parents and adolescents.

Later family life-cycle changes also focus on renegotiation of parent-child boundaries. Children tend to move closer to the executive system following divorce or separation. During this often emotionally charged transitional stage, one child, usually the oldest or opposite gender, tends to take on the identity of the absentee parent. A child who resembles the absentee parent in manner and appearance may become the recipient of parental anger, which is projected onto the child. Such scapegoating can cause a great deal of pain and conflict in parent-child interactions. It can lead to unrealistic expectations of the child's ability to comply, and thus to harsh discipline and punitive parental behavior toward the child. Empathy training to help the parent understand the needs of the child is coupled with helping the mother move out of the victim role and toward greater acceptance and appreciation of the role of single parent. Unfortunately, such resentment toward a child and the absentee parent prevents much collaboration between parents, so that parents who are most in need of support are left to parent alone.

Intergenerational work tends to center on separation issues also. Parents who have difficulty empathizing with the needs of their child for an autonomous existence are likely to have a difficult time making their own needs known to their families of origin. Cross-generational patterns of conflict associated with adolescents' needs for individuation become particularly challenging in the one-parent family, where over-utilization of the parental child in the capacity of coparent becomes problematic.

The term *parental child* is usually employed pejoratively in the family therapy literature, as overreliance on a child to make decisions and to perform parental tasks, such as care of younger siblings, to the extent that peer relations and other developmental needs are sacrificed. Not only in single-parent households but in two-parent families as well, parents are encouraging their children to take on responsibility and to share in performing family tasks. The boundary between the sibling and executive systems becomes more blurred as children increasingly participate in decision making, household tasks, and family responsibilities. Many practitioners have voiced concern that such practices cut childhood short and that children are rushed into adulthood too soon. Clearly, increased responsibility on the part of children in today's families can be both a strength and a potential hazard. In cases where responsibilities interfere with the development of individual autonomy, including peer activities, the practitioner must be a strong advocate for the needs of the children.

REDEFINING FAMILY RITUALS

Declining economic resources tend to create changes in family rituals, such as vacations, dining out, and celebration of important events. The transitional phase following separation or divorce involves reestablishing ways of celebrating important events even in cases where economic resources have not declined significantly. The practitioner helps the family explore alternate ways of marking important milestones through rituals such as local "minivacations" and picnics. Often, family members need to be reminded to focus on the positive elements of change, such as the greater freedom associated with unilateral decision making and less conflictual relationships in the home.

Regularly scheduled family sessions can become part of the important rituals that help establish cohesiveness in the new family structure. The practitioner serves as a teacher and a mediator in helping to establish the participative decision making often found to be prevalent in the mother-headed family (Hartman, 1986). This nonhierarchical process does not eliminate the power of the executive system, but divides that power among family members in a more egalitarian way than is the case in more authoritarian family systems. Democratic problem solving and negotiation skills are strengthened when children are encouraged to bring everyday problems and suggestions up for discussion.

The practitioner can suggest that family members engage in behavioral rehearsal during treatment sessions as a means to enhance listening skills and mutual respect for individual differences of opinion. This process involves practicing how not to interrupt when others speak and taking time to try to understand another's point of view before responding. For example, parents need to have realistic expectations of their children's needs for autonomy. Parental expectations of complete obedience sometimes must be modified from "getting my adolescent to keep his room clean" to "being able to live together for the next two years." Intervention objectives are then reformulated to reflect steps toward resolution of conflicts.

NORMALIZING
THE ADOLESCENT PERIOD

Single parents need to be reminded that although adolescence is not an illness, it is usually a difficult period for all family members. Normalizing this phase of the family life cycle helps to counter the "worried well syndrome" many single mothers exhibit as a result of their internalized negative views about the capacity of mothers to parent alone.

During the adolescence period, parent and child value systems cannot be expected to be in harmony. Some values, such as those concerning the use of drugs, cannot be compromised, however, and these differences can lead to an impasse in the conflict resolution process within the family. Interventions are still focused on the goal of preservation of the family unit, so that the teen can remain at home at least until schooling is completed.

Referrals to self-help groups such as Parenting Together or Tough Love have been helpful to some parents who are experiencing difficulties in defining attainable expectations and holding their teens accountable for their own actions. Support groups offer parents the opportunity to vent feelings of frustration frequently associated with parenting teenagers and letting go of some of the dreams we have for them. It is not unusual for parents to displace their own hopes and aspirations onto their growing children. When compared with the high aspirations parents have for their children's academic achievement and career goals, the harsh reality of a teen out of control is difficult to confront.

FAMILY-PRACTITIONER
CONTRACT AGREEMENTS

A participatory relationship between parent and child allows for the formulation of working agreements that would be difficult to establish in more authoritative family structures. The practitioner can help formulate oral or written working agreements between mother and child. In this case, the agreement is to accomplish objectives leading to the goal of living together until the adolescent completes high school. The working agreement is a contract that specifies expectations of the reciprocal roles of worker and client (Maluccio & Marlow, 1974) or among family members. Contracts comprise jointly formulated goals meeting the criteria of being realistic, attainable, measurable, and time limited (Garvin & Seabury, 1984). The goal, which must be defined clearly, reflects a desired outcome at the end of the intervention period. Measuring the end result of intervention would be difficult if the goal were formulated simply as "getting along better," because we have no agreed-upon definition of "better."

The intermediate goal of reducing shouting from three or four times weekly to once weekly can be helpful in breaking down the sequence of the desired outcome so that success can reinforce step-by-step progress toward the goal. At the end of three months the number of shouting instances can realistically be expected to drop to once per week with the help of intervention. This intermediate goal then leads to an ultimate goal of living together for the next two years. These are outcome goals, reflecting desirable and mutually agreed-upon changes in the clients' lives during and at the end of the treatment sessions, that is, moving toward the ability to live together.

The goal attainment scale (Kiresuk & Lund, 1978) can be used to assess the extent to which outcome goals are accomplished. The scale, originally developed using five categories of goal attainment, can be modified to a three-point level; expected, below expected, and above expected level. The following example outlines mutually formulated expected goal attainment for a family of an adolescent who is at risk of being placed out of the home because of family conflicts:

Above expected level:** (6-month follow-up)
> Teen is residing at home with no support services and manageable conflict level.

Expected level of attainment:**
> Teen is residing at home with help of parent-child support group.

Below expected level:*
> Teen is at risk of being placed out of the home because of family conflicts.
*At intake.
**End of treatment and at follow-up.

Objectives reflect the tasks the client and worker must accomplish in order to meet the desired outcome goal(s). Task attainment is easy to assess because tasks have been accomplished, partially accomplished, or not accomplished within a specific time period. An example of a process agreement leading to the desired outcome of living together for the next two years follows:

> Mother and teen agree to attend family sessions to learn conflict resolution and coping skills. The working agreement between the parent-child dyad interconnects with the practitioner-family contract. The family agrees to participate in an initial six-week session designed to accomplish the following objectives, or tasks, leading to the intermediate goal of reduced shouting and the ultimate goal of living together for at least a two-year period:
> - Mother agrees to respect the adolescent's "space" by not making comments about his room. This agreement begins to firm boundary and

allows teen to make autonomous decision regarding the condition of
his living space.

- Son agrees to engage in one weekly cleaning session of his room, with
specified tasks to be completed and monitored by the practitioner.
This objective is designed to encourage mother to deflect her focus
away from the problematic policing role.
- Mother and son agree to practice listening without interrupting during
treatment sessions. This task is an additional step in creating a firmer
intergenerational boundary where overinvolvement has resulted in
intrusive and problematic communication patterns.
- Both at home and during the weekly treatment session, mother and
son agree to learn to recognize signs of anger and to issue a "time-out"
signal when angry. This objective provides yet another method for
interrupting the pattern of interaction that results in shouting and violent
outbursts.
- Mother and son agree to engage in a forgiveness ritual during treatment sessions. This involves burying past grudges, mutual forgiveness, and a commitment toward empathic understanding of one different point of view during a one-week period.

The practitioner's objectives are to teach the enabling conflict resolution skills and to serve as a mediator of the parent-child conflicts.
Homework assignments can help family members practice these skills
and also provide continuity between the treatment sessions and day-to-
day interactions in the home. Family members can self-report each
week, using a daily chart of the number of successful days when recognizing signs of anger, noninterruptive communication patterns, and room
cleaning served to interrupt the pattern of shouting. This feedback can
help shed light on additional patterns of interactions that have led to
shouting matches during the week.

The contract agreement is likely to need renegotiation at the end of
the six-week period. The formulation of new objectives may include a
referral to a parent-teen support group and other community resources
as well as strengthening family and peer group support systems.

CHANGES IN THE DIVISION OF LABOR

Changes in the division of labor among family members involve re-
assignment of family tasks to minimize the burden on the parent, who
often is the sole provider of family resources. Children as young as 4
and 5 years of age can perform simple household tasks such as picking

up and dusting. The practitioner helps the mother to use contract negotiation as a means of allocating increased responsibilities as the children grow older.

A written consensual agreement between mother and child sets out tasks to be performed and reward systems based on tokens and other reinforcements that are both affordable for the family and desired by the children. These contracts need to reflect realistic expectations of family members' ability to carry out tasks and must be flexible enough to leave room for renegotiation. A 13-year-old, for example, may contract to do the laundry and some housecleaning, but should not be expected to perform most of the household chores.

TIME MANAGEMENT

Time management involves careful weighing of the costs and benefits of many of the functions performed by mothers in more "traditional" families. If such tasks prove to be too costly in terms of energy expenditures, the practitioner needs to give the mother permission to cease performing some household tasks. Mothers who tend toward perfectionism need to be reminded that many chores can be eliminated without dire consequences to the family's well-being. Pastry baking and coupon cutting may stretch the family dollar, and this is often imperative in the one-parent home, but the mother herself must make careful decisions about the worth of each chore in terms of benefit to the family and expenditure of time.

Reduction of such tasks as ironing and changing the bed linens less than once per week can be reframed as energy-saving devices rather than sloppy housekeeping. Time management requires that the advice of well-meaning family and friends about the role of the "good mother" be dismissed and the mother be empowered to draw firm boundaries around her decision-making capacities. Studies have found that mothers who have difficulty giving up some of the tasks they performed before becoming employed full-time risk role overload, stress, and burnout (Krausz, 1986).

Redefining the "good mother" role becomes necessary in later stages of the family life cycle as the mother moves into an advisory role and family members increasingly participate in decision making regarding daily activities and chores. The sole caregiver/wage earner who is torn between career goals and the needs of her family must be reminded that the best parent is the one who encourages self-reliance and sufficiency while making herself available for needed emotional support. Attentive listening, encouraging, and communicating hope and acceptance are social work skills applicable to the nurturing parental role as well.

Emotional support is particularly relevant during the transition following divorce, because changes in the division of labor within the family sometimes result in overreliance on an older child to serve as a parental child. During the individuation phase of development, when adolescents are striving to carve out an autonomous existence, the problem of children maintaining the role of coparents often resonates throughout the system. The following case vignette illustrates how a practitioner may successfully intervene in such a scenario.

Betty W. sought counseling for her daughter Julie, age 11. Ms. W., who had been divorced for 5 years, was the mother of three children, all of whom lived with her. Julie had always posed the most difficulties for her mother, but recently the situation had escalated. Julie was having behavioral problems at school and was belligerent at home. Ms. W. felt at a loss to control her daughter and complained of Julie's fighting, temper tantrums, and argumentative behavior.

The whole family was seen in the initial interview. Julie was the youngest in a sibship of two females and one male. The eldest was 18-year-old Cindy and the second was 14-year-old Mat. The children's father was involved to the extent of taking the children to his home every other weekend and for one month in the summer. He paid child support, but not enough to ease the financial strain on Ms. W. significantly.

The structure of the family depended very much upon the cooperation of Cindy in the role of coparent. This arrangement helped Ms. W. to be employed. Cindy, however, was beginning to resent the time that this cost her and felt that she was sacrificing her social life. Julie "hated" her sister's bossiness and complained that she was a tyrant when Ms. W. was absent. It was clear that Ms. W. also used Cindy as a friend and confidante.

There were many developmental issues in the family. Cindy was finishing high school and was planning for college away from home. Ms. W., who had finished college two years previously, was now about to be promoted to a supervisory position at work. Her new position would require her to travel occasionally and would take her away from home for longer periods. None of the children welcomed this; all of them worried about her being away. Julie was particularly upset about the idea. Ms. W., on the other hand, wanted the opportunity and felt proud of her own achievements. She felt somewhat dismayed about the lack of support from her family.

The practitioner hypothesized that the problems for work centered on transitional and life-cycle issues—fears and perceived losses. Julie's difficulties were clearly linked to her role as the barometer of the family. Interventions involved confronting and grieving the loss of the father, and then the decreasing roles of Cindy and her mother as supportive executive family members. The second part of the intervention identified the family structure as binuclear, with the father playing a more active role in coparenting. Increased paternal responsibility was not seen as minimizing maternal authority and competence. Moving Mat, the other male, into a more responsible role, with added tasks and decision-making capacity, was followed by strengthening the supportive function of the two younger members of the sibling subsystem. The capacity of Julie's peer system to provide support was assessed, as well as the availability of extended family members to serve in a more supportive capacity. Julie did not have any close friends. Creating a new peer support system was seen as an ultimate goal to be pursued after the initial family problems were stabilized. Support of extended family members was strengthened to relieve the overburdened coparental executive system.

The more contextual nature of the interventions included enlarging the target system to include Ms. W.'s work environment and finding ways to coordinate her work schedule so that it was more compatible with her caregiver responsibilities. With careful planning, Ms. W. was able to reestablish a pattern of spending special time alone with Julie and with Mat, and to reinforce Julie's successful approximation to the desired goal of decreased acting-out behavior in school and at home. Firming the cross-generational boundaries between Ms. W. and Cindy was accomplished in tandem with strengthening of the mother's extrafamilial support systems, so that her needs for friendship and confidantes could be met through her peer system.

Chapter 3

CONVERSATIONS AND CONSULTATIONS WITH SINGLE MOTHERS AND THEIR FAMILIES

This chapter continues discussion of ways to implement gender-sensitive premises into practice that is sensitive to the realities of female-headed families. How does a practitioner create a context that, for example, validates the single-parent family as a legitimate and functional family form? How can a practitioner put aside his or her own views in the interest of learning of the experience of these families through *their* eyes? Interestingly, many helping professionals working with families are asking the same kinds of questions with respect to all clients. Social constructivism and feminist and narrative theories have sharpened practitioners' appreciation of the significance of social context in the lives and problems of clients. Out of this has come an increased respect for the client's perception of reality and an emphasis upon empowerment of individuals and families throughout the therapeutic process. Practitioners have been challenged to create practice approaches and techniques that are congruent with new theoretical perspectives. As we shall see, many have responded.

This chapter examines the relevance of the theoretical and practice shifts discussed above for implementing the principles of gender-sensitive practice with mother-headed families. For example, there has been a significant change in conceptualization of the therapist-client relationships. Lynn Hoffman (1985) suggests that therapists "shed power" and view themselves as consultants rather than as therapists. In this vein, the interview, a basic tool, becomes a conversation among equals. We believe that terms such as *conversation* and *consultation* befit the gender-sensitive approach espoused in this book. This shift in language opens the way to empowerment of single mothers by encouraging them to name their own experiences rather than have their experiences defined through labels and diagnoses imposed by professionals. The primary focuses of this chapter are the stance and role of the practitioner and a selection of techniques that can promote change-oriented conversation between the practitioner and members of mother-headed families.

PRACTITIONER'S STANCE
IN THE INTERVIEW

The techniques presented in this chapter are built upon a collaborative stance that invites clients to participate as partners in the endeavor. The theories cited above challenge the notion of the practitioner as an objective observer of reality who possesses the one truth against which dysfunction and progress toward health can be measured. It is recognized that what the therapist observes is very much influenced by the theoretical, cultural, and gender lenses through which he or she views the world.

In many ways, therapists do not discover but invent realities about their clients and their clients' worlds. The world is one of multiple realities, in which it is possible for many voices to be heard and to have power. Gone is the hierarchical expert-client structure inherent in traditional professional relationships. This is not to say that therapists do not bring expert knowledge and valuable experience to the process. What they bring, however, is a partial truth and a willingness to hear and be changed by the client's partial truth. As Minuchin and Fishman (1981) have commented, we must realize that truth is not only unknowable, but always partial.

From the collaborative stance, the interview is seen as a powerful conversation in a "coevolving" process (Hoffman, 1985). New theoretical perspectives emphasize language, perception, and meaning in the evolution and solution of problems. The therapist becomes a "participant observer" (Anderson & Goolishian, 1988) of the therapist-client system. "Through conversations the therapist invites clients to become observers of their own reality, to understand patterns of belief and

behavior in relation to the perceived problem and to explore alternatives" (Pasick & White, in press). There is room for many opinions when
the problem definition does not have to fit neatly into the therapist's hypotheses. The "story" becomes one among many. Real (1990) suggests
that practitioners need not necessarily agree at all times with all views,
may choose at times to share their views, and should always be respect-
fully engaged with the multiple realities that greet them. A major role
of the therapist is to keep the dialogue flowing among all who have an
interest in the problem, in order to generate new options and solutions.

Many single mothers, as we note elsewhere in this book, come for
help feeling judged as deficient and as though no one has listened to
them. The practitioner who operates from the stance recommended here
is actively curious about and respectful of how the single mother and
her family make sense of their world, their problems, and their solutions.
The family gains the sense of empowerment that comes with finding its
voice and having that voice heard.

Practitioners who take this stance are sensitive to the social context
of problems presented by single mothers and their families. They
become acutely aware of the effects of professional helpers and external
systems in generating "problem" language around events when single
mothers are involved. They are more likely to bend every effort to
include representatives of external systems in the therapeutic system in
ways suggested in Chapter 4.

Another significant aspect of the change in the practitioner's stance
in dialogues with single mothers has to do with the development of a
resource orientation. A focus on strengths takes center stage when
therapy is seen as a collaborative arrangement. As Karpel (1986) points
out, "Compared with a primary mission to identify pathology, this stance
increases a therapist's ability to identify and utilize resources" (p. 176).

THE "EDGES" OF THE CONVERSATION

Where to focus the communication with any family is a complex
question, given the multiple facets of family life. This matter may be
further complicated with families headed by single mothers because of
the special issues facing them. Such issues include, for example, relationships with external systems and with the noncustodial parent.
Hoffman (1985) has provided a useful conceptual tool that can aid the
practitioner and the family to find the right focus at the right time. It is

called a "time cable," and it defines potential focal points that might be addressed in the course of therapy.

The time cable is employed in conjunction with the idea of the "presenting edge," which is that "area of most tension and energy between therapist and family" (Hoffman, 1987, p. 50). The edge may shift from one session to the next or within one session. One of the practitioner's jobs, as guide, is to be alert to signals from the family, from within him- or herself, and from others involved in the situation. The edges are not located only in the family but in the therapist, the agency setting, the referral source, and others. Feedback from any of these sources may indicate that the current focus is correct or that a change is indicated. When the edges go unattended and the therapist follows his or her own agenda exclusively, the family may seem "resistant" and the therapy may fail.

The possible edges of these special conversations can be thought of in spatial or temporal terms. Most therapists and families traverse the "time" edges of past, present, and future during the course of their meetings together. In the beginning sessions, the mother-headed family, as well as most families, is focused on the present stress. As the conversations proceed, past events, such as divorce and its effect on family members, come into focus. It is important to consider questions such as the following: What has changed most about the family since the divorce? Who is most upset by the changes? Who believes that the divorce has something to do with present problems? These questions tap into the personal meaning of this major event in the lives of family members. Individuals may for the first time be able to share their perceptions and feelings in ways that are beneficial for the whole family.

Another edge from the past that can have special significance for understanding how a woman experiences being a single parent has to do with her family of origin. Questions about how her family heritage affects her parenting, her view of herself as a woman, and her perception of single-parent families provide a frame of reference for understanding her attitudes about and approach to single parenthood. Discussions about what she learned about parenting from her parents, how she wants to be the same as or different from her parents, and what attitudes and models of single parenting she encountered in her childhood help the single mother recognize the power of the past in her present life. Through this kind of process, the single mother is often able to sort out helpful versus detrimental messages from her past. She and her family may become better able to define their own experience as a single family in ways that work for them.

A conversational search through intergenerational history can sometimes surface resources and inspirational family stories. In answer to a question about whether there were single mothers in her family background, Mrs. P., a newly divorced woman, spoke of a maternal aunt who had raised two children alone following a divorce. For some reason unknown to Mrs. P., her parents had little to do with her aunt after the divorce. Mrs. P. herself had just gone along with the family description of her aunt as "different." As she took a fresh look at her aunt through the eyes of a single parent, she saw a rather heroic figure. In a time when society was even less tolerant of single mothers than it is now, her aunt had found a job in a factory in order to support herself and her children. Mrs. P. decided to renew contact with her aunt to learn more of her story. The aunt was surprised but pleased to share her experience and, in time, a mutually supportive relationship blossomed between the two women.

A journey into future time with the family can also prove fruitful. Later in this chapter, we demonstrate how such a trip can help establish goals, identify obstacles to change, and often produce creative alternatives. Other focal points can be thought of as spatial in that they have to do with relationships, sometimes within the family and sometimes between the family and external systems. In one meeting, family dynamics may be the most productive area for discussion. In others, tension in the relationship between the family and the practitioner and/or the agency may need to be addressed. Sometimes, the therapeutic process cannot proceed until issues related to others who have an interest in defining and resolving the problem are resolved. Each of these areas has the potential to damage the partnership between the family and the therapist and to impede change if ignored.

Most practitioners find themselves immediately drawn to a focus on family dynamics as they begin to communicate with their clients. This is understandable and, of course, necessary. There is danger, however, to the process of engagement and change if crucial but less compelling areas are neglected in talking with single mothers and their families about their lives and problems. For example, for reasons addressed elsewhere, single mothers, who often feel disempowered anyway, may be particularly threatened by a referral for help. They will quite naturally take a great interest in learning what the practitioner is "up to" before freely engaging in talk about their families.

The practitioner can begin to ease the concerns of the single mother by demonstrating sensitivity to possible tension about the referral itself. The initial conversation can be directed to how the single mother is experiencing being told that she or a family member has a problem requiring outside help. What does this mean in terms of the family's sense of competence and self-esteem? Does the family agree with the problem definition and with the idea that outside help is necessary? What are their expectations in this situation? What do they believe the family needs at this point? These kinds of questions convey the practitioner's desire to listen to the family's story about its problems and needs. They are meant to invite the family to full and equal participation in the helping process.

Chapters 4 and 6 make the case for the importance of sensitivity to external systems and their impact upon the mother-headed family. Suggestions are made in those chapters for communicating with the family at that edge, so those will not be repeated here.

There is a "presenting edge" that characterizes each meeting between the therapist and the client. It is less likely that the helping process will become "stuck" when the practitioner pays careful attention to finding and responding to that edge. The remainder of this chapter is devoted to a discussion of some methods and techniques that help keep conversations with single mothers and their families flowing in the direction of understanding and change.

CIRCULAR QUESTIONING

One of the most effective means for creating an atmosphere of respect and collaboration between the mother-headed family and the consulting practitioner is circular questioning. This is a method of creating curiosity within the family and therapy systems (Cecchin, 1987). Circular questions allow the practitioner to gain an understanding of family relationships through the eyes of the family members. Such questions are an invitation to the expression of the multiple perspectives that are vital to understanding family systems and to bringing about change.

One of the most important aspects to address in conversations with a single-parent family is how that family has organized itself to meet its special situation. For example, a simple but good question to pose to each family member is, What has been the biggest change for you since your father (husband) moved out? This elicits a range of views, some positive and some negative. Some family members will mention having too much responsibility, one may worry that the mother must work too much, and others may express anger about the disruption in their lives and lack of money. Depending upon the situation, some family members may voice relief that fighting and abuse have ceased. In any case, these answers can lead to a full discussion of how each person has experienced the relationship and role changes inherent in becoming a single-parent family.

In a way, the process of circular questioning helps family members explain to themselves how an event such as divorce or the death of one parent has changed their relationships and their lives. It provides a way to tap into the family at the level of how being a single-parent family is unique for them. Many families do not engage in this kind of conversation on their own. Through the right questions, the practitioner may trigger a deeper understanding of how each person perceives the problems and the promises of being part of a mother-headed family. One young child, for example, voiced her sadness that her parents' divorce meant that she would be divorced from her paternal grandparents. She felt that they were angry with her mother and would not want to see her, either. She had not revealed her private story of the effects of the divorce until the practitioner asked the family members to talk of their biggest worries about the future. As talking proceeds in this purposeful way, family members are encouraged to listen to each other's perceptions of what it is like to live in this family. They voice their ideas about needed changes and ways to change. The family may begin to experience its multiple perspectives as a resource for future problem solving.

Circular questioning is entirely compatible with the feminist principle of a collaborative relationship between the client and the practitioner. "In the circular interview, the practitioner adopts the attitude of an explorer in the family members' belief system and the consequent interaction patterns" (Ferrier, 1986, p. 28). It is through circular questioning that the therapeutic system consisting of clients and therapist "coevolves" in the direction of change. In line with the goal of keeping the conversation flowing, the practitioner generates meaningful questions based upon the feedback and emerging information from the clients. In other words, client and worker lead each other. The practitioner suspends his or her own opinions and theories for the present, in the interest of learning how the clients make sense of the world and their situation. Circular interviewing is focused on the voices of the clients.

Most circular questions are designed to bring out differences or changes in relationships between people or between people and events. There are many types of such questions; these are best demonstrated through a case example. A single mother, Cynthia D., brought her three daughters—17-year-old Connie, 12-year-old Pam, and 10-year-old Andrea—for counseling. The presenting problem was described as constant fighting among the girls and Pam's deteriorating school performance.

In the beginning, it is usual to ask about the different views of the presenting problem. The therapist also employs questions that may reveal family alignments. The following is an excerpt from the initial interview, after the mother had expressed her primary worry, which was her perception of escalation in fighting:

Therapist: Who agrees with Mother that fighting is a serious problem in this family?

Connie: I do except I'm not the one who fights. And anyway it is more of a problem for me than for her.

Therapist: Why is that?

Connie: Because I'm the one who has to handle it. She's at work. I'm supposed to be in charge but then they fight and when I try to stop it, they get mad at me.

Therapist: Cynthia, what do you think about Connie's view of the problem?

Mother: Well, she's right. I do depend on her when I'm away. I have to work but maybe I didn't realize how hard it is for her sometimes. She doesn't complain much.

Therapist: Maybe later Connie will talk more of what it is like for her. But now, Pam, do you agree more with your sister or your mother about the problem?

Pam: Not with either of them. Connie tries to boss us too much. She thinks she is so big. But we can take care of ourselves. I do yell at Andrea when she gets into my stuff and when she won't let me do my homework.

Therapist: Well, this is a family who is not afraid to disagree. What about you, Andrea?

Andrea: I agree with Pam that Connie bosses us too much. When Mom got her new job, Connie just took over. And, Pam should keep her stuff separate from mine. Besides, if Mom would fix up that spare room like she promised, I wouldn't bother Andrea. She thinks she can have the table to herself whenever she is studying.

Mother: I don't have the time I used to have. That's why the room isn't fixed.
                I'm beginning to think my new job has something to do with all of this.

In this segment, the "edge" is the present description of the family
and the concerns that brought them to this situation. Asking "agreement"
questions—instead of simply, What brings you here?—brings forth
meaningful information at several levels. In terms of family structure,
Connie seems to be the "parentified" child who helps out so that her
mother can work outside the home. As the four speak of their view of the
problem, alignments are suggested that may or may not hold up as the
conversation proceeds. Connie aligns herself with her mother and distances herself from her siblings. The two younger daughters find com-
monality in their protests against their older sister. Something of the
family process can be gathered from the freedom with which each person tells her version of the "problem" story. Individual voices seem to
be tolerated in this family, indicating flexibility as a resource.

Circular questions have "the potential of having liberating effects on
the family" (Tomm, 1988, p. 11). The family members are listening to
the answers and often make their own interesting connections as they
are encouraged to share their perceptions of problematic interactions between other members of the family. For example, as Cynthia D. listened
to her daughters, she began to connect the changes brought about by her
new job to the family difficulties. These interviews are characterized
by a lack of interpretive statements from the therapist. In an empowering way, a premium is placed upon the clients' own perceptions and
analyses of emerging information.

The brief segment above suggests several directions for future exploration by the therapist and the family. If the session continues to be
conducted in a circular fashion, family patterns will be further clarified.
For example, in discussing the concerns of the family above, the following questions might be useful:

- Who is most worried about the fighting at home?
- Who is most worried about Pam's grades?
- Who joins so-and-so in these worries?
- Who is most surprised that Connie feels that way?
- What would have to change to make things better?
- Who else agrees that such a change would help?

At some point in the early discussions with a family, the "edge" will become the onset point of the problem. Circular-type questions for the family above might be as follows:

- Who agrees with Mom that her new job has something to do with your problems?
- Who has a different idea?
- What has been the biggest change for you since your mother took her new job?

These questions also elicit differences and contrasts within the family. They can develop new perspectives within the family. For example, in the D. family, Pam and Andrea talked a good deal about how they thought their mother had changed since taking her new job. They worried that she worked too hard, and they missed her because she was not home as much. Connie, however, stated that her life changed more with the divorce of her parents four years ago. She both liked and disliked how important she had become for her mother. The mother, in answer to these questions, expressed to her daughters the dilemmas she felt as a single mother. She spoke of how she thought her having to leave them more on their own these days was hard, but necessary. This conversation triggered new understandings, and they began to create some workable solutions.

It is important to keep in mind that *circularity* refers not just to the circular process in the family but also to the circular process between therapist and family. The practitioner proceeds on the basis of feedback from the family, "going with" the family while continuing to act as a guide to keep the conversation flowing.

FEED-FORWARD QUESTIONS

Peggy Penn (1985) has devised a way of questioning that addresses the future time edge. These questions encourage family members to imagine their lives in relation to one another at some future date. Single mothers sometimes feel trapped by circumstance and are often stuck because of the ways in which they perceive themselves. A "leap to the future" free from the present situation can often help the family generate new solutions and directions.

In the D. family, discussed above, the fact that things would change next year when Connie left for college was mentioned several times. The therapist responded by asking several future-oriented questions, such as these:

- A year from now, when Connie is gone, what do think will be the biggest change for you?
- What is your biggest worry about having Connie leave?
- If Connie is not here to help settle Pam's and Andrea's fights, what will they do?
- Who will take over Connie's responsibilities?

In response to these questions, family members talked of how they would miss Connie. They all thought that she could "hardly wait to leave." Connie was surprised and touched that her sisters would feel sadness about her leaving. She was then able to reveal her own mixed feelings of excitement and anxiety about leaving the family.

Cynthia spoke of her concern about losing Connie's help and did not know how she could provide for her two younger daughters. Pam and Andrea, projected into the future, realized that they would be a year older. They began to come up with some useful ideas about how to take over some of the things Connie now did. They thought that they would just settle their own disputes when they knew Connie would not be there to do it for them. They told their mother about some school programs in which they could participate so that she would not have to worry about them after school. In actual fact, what the family began to realize on their own was that they had problem-solving capacity. In addition, as the mother commented, "If we can do all of this in a year, why can't we do it now?" This discussion contained the seeds of some solutions to current problems as well as to hypothetical future problems.

REFRAMING

Reframing is an empowering technique that is useful with those single mothers whose efforts to change are hampered by their self-blaming attitudes and devaluation of themselves. Reframing is a way of giving new meaning to an event (Fisch, Weakland, & Segal, 1982; Minuchin & Fishman, 1981). It is akin to seeing a glass as half full rather than half empty. It is based upon the belief that multiple explanations and perceptions of the same situation are all "true" explanations. Therapists have found that helping a family to take a fresh look at a problem through the process of reframing can be a powerful facilitator of change.

As we have discussed previously, many single mothers buy into the deficit model of single-parent families perpetuated by societal institutions. They often hold themselves responsible for all the problems of family members. Putting a contextual frame around a single mother's stress can frequently provide a more workable circumstance for change. When the mother's primary explanation for her family's troubles is that she is somehow deficient, it is useful to turn this idea upside down. She might learn, for example, that society is failing her, rather than the other way around. She might be helped to see that, rather than being incompetent, she is a woman who is juggling many pressures in creative way.

The idea of positive connotation (Selvini-Pallazoli, Boscolo, Cecchin, & Prata, 1980) as a way of reframing is particularly powerful with single mothers. This is a technique for giving a positive frame to the organization of the family. Many single-parent families join with society in seeing their kind of family as deviant. Positive connotation is suggested as a way of offering to a single-parent family a view of their family as "right" and good for them. The practitioner can convey to the family that he or she is not here to "fix" the family because it "ain't broke." In some instances, the practitioner may well congratulate family members for having a democratic family that works rather than having to rely on the usual hierarchical structure. In another situation, the therapist may express sincere admiration of a family in which the adolescent children are able to make thoughtful decisions for themselves.

Another way to help the mother-headed family to reevaluate its opinion of itself with respect to other, more traditional, families is to focus on strengths. When a family enters therapy, it is usually concentrating on problem areas. It can be a welcome surprise to be asked to discuss what they would *not* want to change about each other and the family. One family who was given this task came back with such a long list that they questioned why they thought they had problems in the first place.

Mother-headed families who compare themselves unfavorably to others are helped by questions that ask them to think about the advantages of being such a family. In the D. family, described above, all of the girls agreed that they were more independent than their friends. They liked the fact that their mother trusted them to be alone while she was gone. They were proud that their mother asked them their opinions more than their friends' parents did. The mother admitted that sometimes it seemed better not to have to consult with a spouse about her decisions. She was aware, too, that she might never have returned to school and found a career she really enjoyed if she had remained married. The family, in a sense, reframed the situation in a positive light and gained a great deal of confidence in the process.

Another way to facilitate a mother-headed family's appreciation for its own strengths is to remind the family members of their problem-solving experience in past situations. Imber-Black (1986) has pointed out that "all families are problem-solving entities" (p. 148). Families are continually drawing on their own resources to overcome difficulties. The ways in which they do so become so routine that they are often unaware of these patterns. The therapist can activate their awareness by asking questions such as the following:

- How have you solved a recent problem?
- Who did what about that difficulty?
- Who and what has helped you in the past?
- How did you get others to help you then?
- What is there in this family that will help you now?

It is empowering to realize that, no matter how overwhelmed the single mother and her family are feeling now, they have demonstrated some ability to solve problems in the past.

RESTORYING

Many practitioners today are influenced by narrative theory and center therapy on a story metaphor (Allen & Laird, 1991; White & Epston, 1990). Change is conceived of, in part, as a "restorying" of the private stories that so often determine how people live their lives. Interventions built upon the possibilities inherent in such an approach can prove extremely powerful in work with single mothers.

The first step in the process is to surface the wealth of feeling, meaning, and experience that drives thoughts and behavior. The private story of a single mother who heads a family is also a gender story. Her story often contains ideas of failure as a woman because she was unable to hold her marriage together. She may feel that a woman cannot make it without a man or that her family is incomplete if headed by a woman alone. The practitioner can help her to articulate these ideas and to understand how they get in the way of her developing her competence, and acquaint her with the notion that she had little choice in her belief system about herself. She may be helped to face some of the anger that women typically have difficulty expressing. As she does so, she can begin to "reauthor" her life story (White & Epston, 1990).

One single mother, Mrs. Y., who had divorced an abusive husband, entered the helping relationship plagued with self-doubt about her competence as a parent and the "rightness" of her decision to divorce. By all external measures, Mrs. Y. was quite successful in a new job and with her 3-year-old son. Her feelings were being fueled by a family belief system that divorce is immoral and that a woman has the responsibility to make a relationship work. Throughout the divorce process, Mrs. Y. had been under the impression that her mother was sympathizing with her spouse while being extremely critical of her. Both parents had reminded her that she would not be able to provide financially or emotionally for her young son as he grew older.

In the exploration of therapy, Mrs. Y. realized how her gender story was restricting her life and her development as an adult. She explored her mother's "story" of the wife and mother roles. She discovered that her mother had stayed in a very unhappy marriage "for the sake of the children." Mrs. Y. concluded that her mother, too, secretly resented a belief system that required her to forgo her own desires and needs. In that context, Mrs. Y. understood how her decision to "go it alone" might add to her mother's sense of loss about her own dreams and aspirations. This realization not only strengthened her relationship with her mother, but helped her change her view of herself. She spoke of her decision to leave her husband as "courageous" and acknowledged her own subsequent successes. The therapist posed the question, "If you continue to think of yourself in these new ways, how do you think your story of your future will go?" Having already begun the process of "reclaiming her life" (White & Epston, 1990) from a dysfunctional story, she was ready to go on to "reauthor" a more satisfying future life story.

Another restorying technique developed by White and Epston (1990) is called "externalizing the problem." It is particularly useful with single mothers and their families because it locates problems outside individuals and thus quiets blaming voices. With a woman such as Mrs. Y., for example, it is possible to think of her inhibiting belief system as a tyrant whose main goal is to keep Mrs. Y. on "the straight and narrow" path. The practitioner can help her explore how this tyrant is convincing her that she will be a failure, that she has no right to think of her own needs, and that she is not "a real woman" without a man in her life. When she is able to see how her tyrant discounts her competent side with stories of guilt and fear, she can help to cocreate a plan for fighting back. She can be coached in how to talk back to the tyrant, for example. When she is ready, she can be coached to tell the tyrant to "shut up" or to silence it in other ways. She can even bring in allies, in her family or friendship group, to help her generate new ideas for fighting off the tyrant. This technique, based on metaphor and action, can be surprisingly empowering with single parents. It also works well when children are defined as the problem.

The following chapters of this book present various aspects of life in single-parent families that are central to understanding and helping those families. Each chapter discusses an "edge" that may become a critical focus in the work of the practitioner and the family members. The collaborative stance and techniques advocated in this chapter may serve to keep the practitioner and the families with whom they consult on track in their conversations about problems, needs, and change.

Chapter 4

MOTHER-HEADED FAMILIES AND THE EXTERNAL ENVIRONMENT

Gender-sensitive practice with families headed by single mothers is highly contextual. For reasons detailed elsewhere in this book, one priority for practitioners is to understand family problems and needs in the context of stresses originating in the extended environment. Indeed, it is often true that alleviation of stress depends upon family members' relationships with various people and institutions in their larger environment. This chapter draws upon principles from ecological and family-centered practice that are quite compatible with the gender-sensitive approach emphasized throughout this book. The following case example sets the stage for our discussion.

Marjorie M., a 42-year-old single mother with two daughters living at home, was referred for help with 12-year-old Janie. The family had been referred for family therapy by the school social worker because of problems exhibited by Janie at school. Janie had missed many days of school, often refused to attend, and, on several occasions, had left her classroom abruptly, saying that she was sick and had to "get home to Ma." Janie was thought to be a bright child but an underachiever and a very worried child. Both the school social worker and the teacher believed that Janie's difficulties were a reflection of trouble in the family. Callie, Janie's 14-year-old sister, also experienced difficulties in attending school and, in addition, was often in difficulty because of angry outbursts and fighting.

Mrs. M. had been divorced from the children's father for 5 years. He was described as an alcoholic and an abusive man to whom she had been married for 18 years. In addition to her two daughters, Mrs. M. had three adult sons living independently away from her home. John, age 17, had recently married, had an infant son, and lived nearby. Jesse was 20 years old, in the Marines, and stationed in the South. Mike was 23 years old, married with two young children, and lived several miles away from his mother's home. Mr. M., her former husband, had remarried 2 years previously and contributed little to the support of his daughters, although he did continue to have contact with them.

Marjorie M.'s major source of income was from Aid to Families with Dependent Children (AFDC). She had worked as an aide at a nursing home for a brief period, but had to quit when the person upon whom she relied for transportation left her job. Mrs. M. had no car and did not know how to drive. She had few job skills, having married at 18 when she finished high school. She had never worked outside the home during her marriage. Mrs. M. and her daughters lived in a trailer park, where there was little public transportation available. The only means of transportation upon which the family could rely was from John and Mike, and they were not always able to respond immediately. In effect, Mrs. M. and her two daughters were isolated and felt very uneasy and concerned about having no control over this aspect of their lives.

In spite of some very trying environmental pressures, this family had a great deal of strength. They were a close, loyal family who enjoyed being together. The daughters were protective of their mother and very concerned about her well-being. Mrs. M. managed pretty well on her meager financial resources and was motivated to try to find employment. She admitted to some problems in parenting now that her daughters were becoming teenagers, but was open to help in that area. All three family members were worried about Janie's school problems, believing that the family might be separated if Janie did not go to school.

THE ECOLOGICAL PERSPECTIVE

Gender-sensitive practice expands on both ecological and family-centered practice in its attention to the analysis of women's interaction with the external environment. One current emphasis in family-centered practice, for example, is on understanding families and their difficulties in the context of their relationships with larger systems. As

Germain and Gitterman (1980) have pointed out, "People, like all living organisms, together with their environment, form an ecosystem in which each shapes the other" (p. 5). The case presented above illustrates how family stress can be understood from an ecological perspective. Problems are not located exclusively either in the family or in the environment. Rather, they are thought of as the manifestation of tension created by an incongruent fit between the two. This incongruent fit often reflects the family's lack of skills and energy for making effective connections with environmental resources. More important, however, it can reflect the lack of responsiveness to and resources for single mothers and their children on the part of the larger society. When a stressful imbalance exists between the needs of these families and their resources, the explanation lies not only in the family but within larger systems as well.

Almost every writer on families headed by single mothers points to the relationship with the larger environment as a determining factor in the well-being of those families. The "goodness of fit" between a family and its environment depends upon active engagement of family members with such systems as work, schools, health, and recreation. One goal is to empower single mothers to change their environments, and not simply to adapt to inhospitable and sometimes hostile circumstances. Mother-headed families face some special tasks and difficulties in this area primarily because so many are disadvantaged financially and feel powerless.

The ecological metaphor proves to be highly useful in developing an explanatory context around some of the difficulties experienced by families headed by single mothers. An ecologically minded practitioner does not seek a single explanation for a problem or a single source for a solution. Rather, he or she understands the situation in terms of the interconnectedness of social, psychological, physical, and cultural factors. The internal experience of the individual, as well as that person's material well-being, is greatly affected by the quality of connectedness between the family and the outside world. We do not deny the necessity of understanding internal structure and dynamics when the mother-headed family encounters problems. We believe, however, that the problems of the mother-headed family are not so much indicative of deficits in the family structure as suggestive of deficits at the interface of the mother-headed family and larger systems vital to its well-being.

A common source of environmental stress that many mother-headed families share has to do with the negative attitudes they encounter in many quarters of the larger society. Many representatives of societal systems, such as schools, social agencies, churches, and employers, view these families as deficient and "problem saturated" (White & Epston, 1990). This provides a gloomy context against which to project their efforts to achieve a sense of belongingness, normality, and health. Unfortunately, negative judgments originating in the larger society are so pervasive and powerful that members of the families may internalize this "story" of themselves. They often become self-blaming and begin to act in self-defeating ways, thus fulfilling the prophecy from the world outside the family.

In many cases, the first task of the practitioner who consults with these families is to help them find alternative and more favorable views and descriptions of themselves. One way to "restory" their experience is to provide a realistic appreciation of the connection between stress and problems and environmental pressures. A major advantage of the ecological explanation lies in its depathologizing effect. The M. family, for example, found it relieving and empowering when the therapist related their stress to the loss of many external supports in recent years. They had been deprived of financial support from Mr. M. and emotional support as a result of the death of Mrs. M.'s father. Access to needed shopping, health care, recreation, and Mrs. M.'s employment had been severely impaired by loss of transportation. Mrs. M. could also realize that some of the resources her family desperately needed, such as adequate public transportation, did not exist in her community. Explanations such as these helped to diminish Mrs. M.'s belief that her family suffered problems because of her failure as a single mother. She was then able to conceive of solutions in which she played an active and competent part. At one point, for example, Mrs. M. commented, "If I could get a decent job and a car, I think we could be just like other families."

The ecological metaphor is particularly apt for helping mother-headed families because it articulates so well with the principles of feminist-based and gender-sensitive practice. This metaphor presents one way of operationalizing empowerment, networking, and an affirmation of women's experience. Women's developmental experience, for example, places a premium upon connectedness, nurturing relationships, and cooperation (Gilligan, 1982). An ecological approach celebrates these values by associating strength with interdependence and interconnectedness. As a matter of fact, some suggest that the "women's values" described above may, in the long run, present a saner basis for living for both sexes and for family life (Surrey, 1985). The need of the mother-headed family for environmental support is normalized when it is cast in the framework of feminist values. When mother-headed families are affirmed and guided by these values, they are identified with the forefront of changing family life—a most empowering thought.

An ecological perspective working in tandem with feminist principles helps a family clarify its unique experience as a mother-headed family for the benefit of its own members as well as for the helping practitioner. In addition, the way is opened for such a family to identify comforting commonalities with other families. As the family explores its problems, stresses, and resources in the context of its external ecology, it gains an appreciation that they are not alone. They see that all families, not just those headed by single mothers, face the task of constructing an environment in which the family can thrive.

With help from a therapist who is empowerment oriented, the single family may shift its stance from that of passive recipient of the environment to that of active participant in moving toward change.

All of the above suggest that a useful and empowering first step in working with mother-headed families is to focus upon understanding the fit or lack of it between the family and its extended environment. Helping family members gain an understanding of their relationship with the world outside the family boundary can do the following:

- empower through countering the image of mother-headed families as deficient
- normalize their view of problems by relating the stress to expected developmental tasks for families headed by a single parent
- underscore the need for connectedness with a variety of external systems
- mark appropriate connectedness as a strength rather than a sign of weakness
- help identify resources currently supportive to the family and resources that may be activated
- engage the family in a participatory process with the practitioner to make changes in both the family and the environment

MAPPING THE ECOLOGY
OF THE MOTHER-HEADED FAMILY

Family-centered practitioners have developed some visual tools that are helpful for understanding the complexity of a family system and its ecology. Being able to see the multiple layers and interconnectedness of families and external systems provides context and texture to family life and problems. A well-known aid for assessing a family's relationship to significant larger systems is the ecomap.

The ecomap helps family members to visualize themselves in the space of their environmental context. As Hartman and Laird (1983) point out, the ecomap furnishes a holistic view of the family. It identifies resources available, resources missing but needed, areas of stress between family members and other systems such as schools and employers, how well the family is able to carry on transactions with the extended environment, and even something of the inner life of the family. While this technique may be known by many readers, we want to revisit the ecomap for its particular relevance to assessing the needs, strengths, and resources of the mother-headed family.

Ecomapping is a technique very much in keeping with feminist therapists' call for a more egalitarian, less hierarchical relationship between client and helpers. It invites family members to participate in telling the story of their experience as a mother-headed family in relation to a world outside family boundaries. What strengths do family members identify, and where do they find the world inhospitable? In the process, the inner languages and the inner lives of the family members are often revealed to the helping practitioner as well as to themselves. During the course of ecomapping, for example, Janie M., in the family described above, was surprised and impressed to hear her mother talk of her longtime interest in becoming a nurse. The practitioner's role is to keep the conversation flowing and focused on that "edge" between the family and relevant external systems.

Single mothers whose previous experiences have made them wary of would-be helpers usually find the ecomap a nonthreatening and non-blaming beginning. A completed ecomap for the M. family will serve as an example of this tool's usefulness for assessing the needs of, setting goals for, and engaging the mother-headed family (see Figure 4.1).

MAKING AN ECOMAP

For those unfamiliar with the process of ecomapping, we present a short summary (for a more detailed discussion, see Hartman & Laird, 1983). Names of the members of the household are placed within a large circle that marks the boundary between the household and its external environment. Noncustodial parents are connected to the custodial

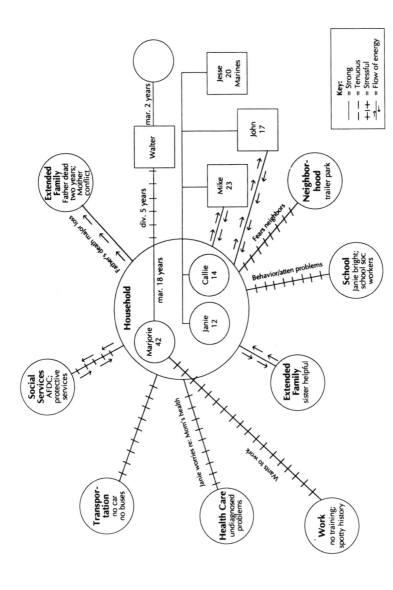

Figure 4.1. The M. Family Ecomap

Key:
—— = Strong
– – – = Tenuous
+ – + = Stressful
⇉ = Flow of energy

Walter
mar. 2 years

Jesse
20
Marines

John
17

Mike
23

Household

Extended Family
Father dead
two years;
Mother conflict

Father's death major loss

div. 5 years

mar. 18 years

Callie
14

Janie
12

Marjorie
42

Fears neighbors

Neighbor-hood
trailer park

Behavior/atten problems

School
Janie bright;
school soc
workers

Extended Family
sister helpful

Social Services
AFDC;
protective services

Transpor-tation
no car
no buses

Janie worries re: Mom's health

Health Care
undiagnosed problems

Wants to work

Work
no training;
spotty history

45

parent, but placed outside the large circle. The small circles represent the external systems that are of significance to the well-being of the family members. The connecting lines indicate the nature and the quality of those connections. The more pronounced the line, the stronger the connection; dotted lines denote tenuous connections. Varying experiences of each family member with the specific external system are shown by separate lines. Descriptive words, elicited from the family, can further illuminate the emerging picture. In the example shown in Figure 4.1, Janie M.'s school experience is distinguished as qualitatively different from Callie's experience.

HOW TO INVOLVE THE FAMILY

Since ecomapping is an easy way to engage all family members, and since it contains clear and graphic information, we recommend that the map be done in the first meeting, if possible. This establishes a partnership atmosphere from the beginning, through the invitation for all voices to be heard in the process. The practitioner serves as a guide, but is only one voice among many. This approach proved to be a positive experience for the M. family, because they had perceived many of their previous encounters with helping professionals as demeaning and controlling. At one point, the therapist commented on how difficult it must be for Mrs. M. to think about working outside the home given the fact that she had centered her life on the care of her children. She replied that this was the first time she felt anyone was listening to her side of the story. When it became clear to the M. family that their ideas carried weight, they were quick to share them.

Single mothers and their families are often able to gain more helpful views of their difficulties by using such holistic maps of their life space. They arrive at connections between problems and circumstances that reframe, or put in more positive perspective, their experiences. This process can then lead to problem solutions. The M. family quickly came to a new understanding of Janie's school problems in light of her worry about her mother's lack of health care and transportation. Discussion of the impact of the father was surprising, as the girls shared their relief that they did not have to worry about their mother being abused any longer. This led them to share other positives about their status as a mother-headed family, such as less conflict in day-to-day interactions among family members.

The family was introduced to the mapping idea in a straightforward manner. It was explained that mothers heading families often face special obstacles in providing for their families, and that a map of the family could help to identify where some of the stress was coming from and what the family had to work with in the way of resources. To elaborate a bit more on the mapping procedure, the practitioner explained that all families must build bridges between themselves and the world outside in order to get needed support. The practitioner then added these comments:

> Some bridges are more difficult to build than others and some are needed where none exist at present. With this map we can all see where you have bridges, where some are not so strong, and where new ones are waiting to be built. Some of you may have bridges that the rest do not have. Maybe one of you has important connections that the others don't even know about. This is the time for everybody to share their ideas about what is already built well and what is needed. There may even be some surprises along the way.

Mrs. M. responded enthusiastically to the ecomap as an expert about her family. The two daughters were easily engaged in this process, as most children are, because it is an easy and usually pleasant way to participate. As they discussed their connections to school, Janie revealed that she often becomes worried about whether "Ma is okay" and that is one reason she leaves her classroom abruptly. It turned out that Mrs. M. was experiencing some health difficulties that concerned all three members of the household. The map revealed inadequate access to health services, in large part because transportation was lacking. Janie pointed out that one thing that would help her feel better about going to school would be for "Ma to learn to drive" and to get a car. She and the rest of the family felt isolated and cut off from the rest of the world. There was an additional interesting interplay between these environmental difficulties and Janie's school problems. Mrs. M. and Janie talked of how they activated Janie's adult brothers' interest by calling them whenever Janie became upset about school. Usually, one of the brothers would drive over to calm Janie by taking the family for a drive. In a sense, Janie's behavior triggered a response pattern that reassured both Mrs. M. and her daughters that they could obtain transportation in the event of a crisis.

Several other crucial environmental stressors emerged during the mapping process, including the relationship between the family and the school. Mrs. M. could not get to school conferences because of transportation problems. Financial resources were at a minimum level, and the family felt at risk and different in their neighborhood because they lived in a trailer park that housed a large number of families from an ethnic group very different from the M. family. Even the language spoken there was one they did not share. It later turned out that there was great potential for connecting with neighbors. At this point, however, the ecomap discussion revealed the family's isolation from the neighborhood environment.

The process of ecomapping proved to be an effective way for Mrs. M. to organize her concerns, goals, and resources. This family discovered that it was not without resources. With respect to resources, Janie said at one point, "I never knew so many people knew us." Callie volunteered, "I'd like to see Aunt Betty more. We used to have fun with her and her kids. She has a car and I bet she would drive us places." Thus the ecomapping session had an empowering effect upon a family who typically viewed themselves as dependent, pathological, and powerless. As Mrs. M. commented, "Now I see why I'm so tired all the time. There is not so much wrong with me, but we need to change some of those marks on the map, I guess." At the end of the first meeting, Mrs. M. commented that she would see to it that a plan was made for Janie to get back to school. She even insisted that their next appointment be held after school hours.

It should be noted from the above discussion that the family needs to be actively involved in the analysis of the ecomap. It is empowering for family members to supply their own interpretations rather than have explanations come from the therapist. In like manner, the family is encouraged to take responsibility for defining goals for change, essentially for describing how they would like their ecomap to look in the future. The ecomap also serves as an ongoing instrument for evaluating progress the family is making in its relationship with the world beyond its boundaries.

For the M. family, the ecomap provided a way to pinpoint some needs and some workable goals, particularly for Mrs. M. Still a young woman, Mrs. M. was encouraged to examine her own future needs as an adult, as the ecomap clearly illustrated few satisfying adult connections in her life. Her life had been centered on being a parent, and she felt a growing sense of failure and fear of loss in that realm, especially because her last two children were growing up. Improving her parenting skills, including boundary setting, became a goal for her, as well as the development of some supportive adult relationships.

Many goals of change had to do with connecting the family to community and extended family resources. One very important change came as the family negotiated with John and Mike for consistent transportation and contact rather than have Janie's problematic behavior be the mediating influence. Another significant intervention came with the assembly of a network of school staff and interested parties from various agencies to arrive at a "helping" plan with this family. Later in this chapter, we show how the practitioner helped to empower Mrs. M. to influence school personnel to make some changes. Other areas addressed were those of obtaining greater financial support from the father and job training for Mrs. M. Mrs. M.'s active participation in making these environmental changes happen reinforced her growing sense of herself as competent and effective mother and woman.

WHAT AREAS TO MAP

There are several areas of sensitivity to be alert to when exploring the mother-headed family's relationship to the external environment. Certainly, ties to the world of work and other sources of income are extremely important. Of course, not all such families are impoverished, but even those women who are providing well for their families are subject to stress at this "edge." For example, professional women who head families often experience stress in the work area as a result of tension between the demands of their jobs and child care. Many organizations are not especially friendly to the idea of a mother leaving a meeting, missing work, or questioning the time and travel required by an assignment. Her dedication to her job and her motivation may be open to doubt and may interfere with promotions and salary increases. And dependable and adequate child care is not always easy to come by, even for those with ample financial means.

As we have documented elsewhere in this book, the M. family represents a common situation, in which the single mother is struggling to gain sufficient income. The M. family's major income source was from AFDC. The father was doing well financially but contributed little. This is not an unusual circumstance; only one-third of single mothers receive child support. Mrs. M. wanted outside employment, but was ill prepared to enter the job market, having spent her adult life in child-rearing activities.

The question, when exploring the employment picture with the family, is not just about "facts," but about how members of the family make sense of this experience at the personal level. In the structured discussion that accompanies ecomapping, the way is opened for understanding the meaning of experience. Such understanding can often form a basis and a direction for change. Mrs. M., for instance, felt incompetent and powerless about job possibilities. She had little hope for change, and her attitudes were reinforced by the larger society. This affected her daughters' view also, not only of her, but of themselves as females. No one affirmed Mrs. M. for her contributions and value in the mothering she had done all of those years. During the process of ecomapping, however, the therapist took the opportunity to make a positive comment about Mrs. M.'s efforts as a mother. The thought was planted that perhaps her competence and commitment in the realm of parenting could be transferred to employment outside the home.

In the case of another client, a professional woman with a high income, the "meaning" issue around work that emerged in the course of the ecomap discussion was completely different from Mrs. M.'s situation. This client was very successful in her career but denigrated herself for "neglecting" her son because of all the demands on her time in the work world. She was admittedly ambitious and enjoyed the mark she was making in her career. Her son's father was uninvolved and his whereabouts unknown. She expressed her problem:

> I am so tired of rushing. I rush from my work to Tim's school and back to work again. There are evening meetings for his activities and reports for me to write at night for the next day at work. Tim complains that we don't do any fun things any more. My boss complains that I seem distracted from my work. I don't know what to do. There is no one to help.

This woman's dilemma and frustration were in many ways just as stressful as, although different from, Mrs. M.'s.

The relationship between school and the family is another area fraught with potential stress for all members of families headed by mothers. Dornbusch and Strober (1988) note that single parents are less likely to engage in school-related activities because of time pressures. They go on to state that when single parents are perceived by school personnel as less interested or less active, both teachers and the children are affected. Teachers begin to believe that these children will do less well in school, and they do—a vicious circle. Interestingly, however, the same study shows that when teachers try to develop partnerships with parents, single mothers prove to be eager to cooperate and children's grades improve. It certainly seems indicated for helping professionals to do some work at this edge by including school personnel in the therapeutic system. Among other things, parent-school conferences can be initiated. Mothers can be empowered to visit their children's schools and can be helped to learn more effective ways of interacting with teachers and other school personnel.

Each family has its own sensitive spots with the environment, and each has its own set of resources. The practitioner cannot fully predict which to include. As a matter of fact, the goal is to activate the family to take responsibility as much as possible. Certainly, however, it is important to identify who is in the support network to whom the family turns for material and emotional support. Particular attention should be given to resources available to the mother for her own social needs and support. Other significant areas to explore with mother-headed families include connections with noncustodial parents and with extended family. Because these topics are covered at length in later chapters, they will not be discussed here.

"MEANING" AND MOTHER-HEADED FAMILIES

Michael White, an innovative thinker and clinician in the field of family therapy, has proposed that rather than some underlying structure or dysfunction in the family, "it is the meaning that members attribute to events that determines their behavior" (White & Epston, 1990, p. 3). The conversation that builds around the ecomapping process affords the therapist access to the family's world of meaning about being a mother-headed family. This, in turn, may provide some clues about some of their behavior for the enlightenment of the helping practitioner as well as for the family itself.

The central event of being a mother-headed family does not represent the same reality for everyone. As the map of the household is drawn, there is opportunity to help the family reflect on the circumstances that led to its joining the ranks of similar families. Was this family formed through divorce or by the death of the father? Did the mother who heads this family make a choice to form a family as a single parent? Is she the biological parent or an adoptive parent? How do the children in the family understand the circumstances? Are there unresolved issues reflected in the comments? How do children make sense of a divorce, for example? What is it like for each person to be a member of a family headed by a single mother?

One way to gain an understanding of the meaning of an event is to listen to people talk of the perceived impact upon their lives. In the case of death or divorce, a useful question is, What is the biggest change in your life since your father/husband left/died? Often this will spark a lively and informative discussion among family members, especially when there are discrepancies in the answers. Differences are not always perceived in negative terms, such as decreased income or emotional loss. With the M. family, for example, all three family members felt safer with Mr. M. out of the home, because he had been abusive with all of them.

People "story" their lives every day as they try to explain the events of their lives in a meaningful way. As the ecomap is developed, thoughtful questions can facilitate the telling of stories about what it means to be a mother-headed family in relation to the larger world outside. Questions such as the following tap into meaning and story:

- How do think your family is doing in comparison to other families in the neighborhood?
- How do you think your family is different from families with two parents in the home?
- Do you think the school people would talk with you differently if the children's father lived here?
- In general, would any of these marks on the ecomap be different if there were two parents living in this home?

As each external system is discussed, similar "meaning" questions can help family members reveal their sense of identity in the outside world. Basically, these questions are meant to surface the family's perception of itself in relation to the outside world. How do they think they are perceived? What is their explanation for how the world perceives them? How closely are their explanations linked to their status as a mother-headed family? One message single mothers often report hearing from people outside the family is, "Your family really needs a father to . . .". The meaning to the mother and her children is usually that their family is incomplete and deficient. When this arises in the ecomap discussion, it is important to determine who in the family, including the mother, agrees with this message. If the level of agreement is high and this meaning deeply embedded, measures can be taken to help the family develop more functional perceptions of themselves as a family.

Unfortunately, for many women, to be a single parent means to be powerless. They are often powerless to enforce agreements with ex-husbands for child support or visitations. They may feel powerless in efforts to secure adequate employment and child care. They may feel inadequate in their dealings with employers, teachers, principals, physicians, and even their extended families. Some even feel that they are not taken seriously by mechanics hired to repair their automobiles. The feeling of not being able to influence the environment can contribute to a sense of hopelessness.

The process of ecomapping will usually reveal the single mother's feeling of helplessness as she discusses the conflicts and stresses she experiences with various external systems. The kinds of questions that can help focus the discussion include the following: When do you feel you were listened to by [name]? Who is easiest for you to talk to about this? Who do you think would take you seriously about [a given topic] at the school? Who could help you get the money your husband owes? Beyond this, the practitioner can ask questions that begin to suggest that other systems external to the family need to change. For example, How do you think the school could be more helpful to you in this situation? What are your needs in this situation, and what support do you need to get your employer to listen to you? These questions may introduce a surprising new thought to the single mother who is not accustomed to articulating her needs because of negative responses.

ENLARGING THE THERAPEUTIC SYSTEM THROUGH ECOMAPPING

"The problem is the meaning system created by the distress and the treatment unit is everyone who is contributing to the meaning system. This includes the treating professional as soon as the client walks in the door" (Hoffman, 1985, p. 387). In other words, every problem creates a system of interested parties who contribute to the problem definition from their various perspectives. The ecomap can serve to define this "problem-determined system" and to enlarge the therapeutic system. Since the problems of mother-headed families are frequently defined and exacerbated by larger systems, direct contact with representatives of those systems is warranted. Such contact gives a more complete picture of the family and its problems. More important, larger systems can often be enlisted into a problem-solving partnership with the family.

Imber-Black (1988), who has written a great deal about the relationship between families and larger systems, notes the necessity of determining which larger systems are actively involved with the family and what problem definitions about the family exist. One reason for this is the possibility for larger systems to place problem-solving constraints upon the family through their perceptions and value impositions. The ecologically minded practitioner can be of enormous help to the single mother by fostering more positive perceptions of her and her family within relevant larger systems. The aim is to facilitate a dialogue in which the mother's story and reality are respected. In a sense, the role of the therapist who is working at the boundary between family and external systems is to shift the conversation so that the "problem-determined system" is transformed into a problem-solving system.

Larger systems can contribute to problems of mother-headed families in many ways, some of which are quite subtle. Imber-Black (1988) discusses the mixed and binding messages communicated to women clients from representatives of larger systems. Women are given the responsibility for handling stressful issues of family members and are simultaneously criticized for initiating and maintaining patterns of enmeshment. Mothers are often contacted and engaged by larger systems, multiple helpers, and referral systems that highlight deficits rather than strengths and identify specific helpers for every problem. Imber-Black goes on to point out that if the woman cooperates as the conduit for implementing all the referrals, she is often characterized as over-involved. If she does not follow through, she is thought of as resistant.

When larger systems share a deficit-model view of mother-headed families, they often encourage the single mother to rely on those systems to become the missing parent. She is often given the message that helping professionals can care for her children more competently than she can. None of this serves to enhance her strengths and to affirm and empower her in her parent role. This kind of undermining, subtle or not so subtle, often places children in an untenable position, too. They can be caught between the mother and well-meaning helpers from powerful systems outside the family.

Clearly, it is important to include these systems in assessment of the family and its problems and to try to enlist them as resources for the family. This can be done in several ways. One is to help the family learn how to deal with these systems in new and powerful ways. When the single mother can do this on her own, it underscores a growing sense of competency. For example, in the M. case, Mrs. M. was coached about how to talk with teachers and with her welfare worker to make her needs and desires known in a more productive way. She was helped to find ways to make her environment more responsive.

It is preferable but not always possible for the mother to fend for herself with larger systems, for a variety of reasons. She may lack the skills and confidence in the beginning. Sometimes it is useful for the practitioner to be in direct contact with representatives of larger systems for the sake of clarity and support, and to reframe the family in a positive light. We recommend joint meetings with appropriate family members, representatives of significant larger systems, and the helping practitioner early in the course of work with the family. Such meetings can help to clarify the roles and expectations of everyone involved and thereby clear away confusion.

The practitioner takes responsibility for setting up a meeting, and for preparing family members to take part. Family members often need to be helped to think through their goals, areas that need clarification, how to present their views, and questions to ask. Sometimes, the therapist can serve as a coach and can help the family to rehearse. Premeeting preparation includes the following:

- enlisting family participation in identifying members of larger systems who should attend the meeting
- helping the family to identify areas of confusion in the relationship with the larger system
- helping the family to frame questions they would like to have answered at the meeting
- rehearsing family in presenting their points at the meeting, if necessary
- helping the family to ask for changes in and support from the larger system

The practitioner is responsible for conducting the meeting, but not controlling it. It helps to think of the meeting as an opportunity to enlarge the therapeutic system and to develop a conversation of change within that system. An emphasis on goals and alternative courses of action helps promote the possibility of change on the part of the larger systems as well as on the part of the family.

It is most important that an atmosphere of respect for multiple views be established. In the case of the M. family, the family therapist arranged a meeting with Mrs. M. and the school personnel involved with the daughters. Those in attendance included a school social worker, teachers, the principal, the school psychologist, and a school counselor. The therapist started by saying, "In my talks with Mrs. M., I've found her very concerned about Janie's missing school and she has some very interesting ideas on the subject. But, both Mrs. M. and I would find it very helpful to hear what you think, since you see Janie in school and probably have some helpful thoughts." This served to establish Mrs. M. as an equal and interested participant who had something to offer but wanted to learn at the same time. The way was opened for negotiation around the problem and for reframing it in a more useful way. As Mrs. M. was able to articulate her concerns, the school personnel were able to consider other problem definitions than that of a child from a family headed by a disinterested, overwhelmed, and incompetent mother.

Carefully planned and executed meetings between the family and larger systems can go a long way toward easing the nonproductive tension that may exist in these relationships. That was certainly the case in the meeting between the school personnel and Mrs. M. As the school people were able to see Mrs. M. in a different light, she gained confidence and began, with some prompting from the family therapist, to talk of some of her ideas about what would help. She talked of Janie's fears about her, Mrs. M.'s, health. She wondered whether it would be possible, at least for a short time, to allow her daughter to make phone calls home to assure herself that her mother was all right. She knew that this action would not solve everything, but thought it would help to keep Janie in school for the present. The teachers and the principal readily agreed. The principal added that he thought he could also arrange for Callie, the older daughter, to have a part-time job helping in the office. This was offered out of concern for ways to help build Callie's self-esteem and interest in school attendance. Others contributed useful ideas as the system converted itself to a team working toward solutions together. Mrs. M. left this meeting feeling empowered and much more competent with respect to her abilities to handle future relations with this particular larger system.

Some of the most fruitful meetings with systems in the single mother's environment are those with her extended family. Nurturing connections between members of the nuclear family and maternal grandparents, maternal siblings, and other kin can be strong and valuable resources for everyone. Meetings that focus on fostering such connections are powerful and need careful planning, especially when communication has been partially or totally cut off. Chapter 5 covers this important topic in detail.

Chapter 5

SUPPORT FROM
FAMILY AND PARTNERS

Mother-headed families are in need of various types of support, including emotional, informational, and task support, as well as financial assistance. Extended family members provide task support when they baby-sit as a way of temporarily relieving an overburdened young mother of her child-care responsibilities. Such respite child care, emergency financial assistance, and information about how to take care of a baby's basic needs are as important as emotional support or having someone to talk to about problems. The single parent tends to lack both the financial resources and respite child care necessary to engage in social interactions with peers. The combination of not being able to get away to talk with other adults and time constraints, resulting from the dual roles of caretaker and wage earner, leave many single women isolated from needed emotional support and vulnerable to depression (Gold & Milner, 1983).

Social support is defined as help that is available in difficult or stress-arousing situations (Sarason & Sarason, 1982) and feeling valued and belonging to a group (Cobb, 1976). Network interventions are aimed at maximizing utilization of extended family support, including not over-utilizing support in such a way as to minimize the ability of extended family members to provide ongoing support. The goals of network intervention, therefore, center on resolving conflicts and facilitating negotiations within the mother-headed family, including partners, children, and extended family.

The sharing of parental responsibilities is a central issue in network interventions where partners and absentee fathers are seen as important parts of a strong support network. These types of interventions are focused toward strengthening the capacity of the family to seek and to utilize support and to set out expectations and commitments to sharing the responsibility for child rearing.

Absentee fathers must be seen as potential sources of support. The ideal view of partner support is the concept of the single-parent family as binuclear, with the absentee parent sharing caregiving responsibilities to the extent of coparenting. This type of arrangement deserves further elaboration, and is discussed at length in Chapter 10.

Partners who are a part of the household in cohabiting, "blended," or "reconstructed" families, can certainly be encouraged to share responsibilities for child rearing. Even a partner who has a more tenuous relationship with the family can be expected to take some part in financial and child-care obligations. Although most partners are male, we discuss special problems encountered by the more than a million children who live in families where the mothers' partners are also women. Because partner support is so critical to a strong support network, the gender-sensitive practitioner advocates raising expectations that live-in partners and absentee fathers have a strong role in providing financial, task, and emotional support for children whenever possible. The combination of absentee parent, partner, and extended family support can make the difference between an overburdened mother-headed family and a family capable of supporting, nurturing, and socializing children.

MEDIATION OF
INTERGENERATIONAL CONFLICTS

Strengthening support from extended family may require intergenerational work and interruption of established patterns of parenting over several generations. The size of the support network, or how many people are available for help, is the first step in network assessment, followed by how often help is provided when needed. Tracy (1990) has found some evidence that single parents perceive less support and experience more conflicted networks than do other parents. Network interventions thus often must be targeted toward resolving conflicts related to lack of compatibility between the needs of the mother-headed family and the help offered by potentially helpful network members.

Because of rapid changes in the structure of the family over the last two decades, this compatibility is often difficult to achieve. The number of divorces has more than doubled over the past two decades, and the number of children living with one parent has increased 250% since 1960 (U.S. Bureau of the Census, 1989a). The increase in one-parent households can result in a single parent's receiving advice and suggestions based on her mother's experience in a two-parent system. Such suggestions may not fit very well with the life-style of the mother-headed family.

The rapid increase of women in the labor force during the past two decades, for example, increases the likelihood that a daughter differs from her mother in level of participation in the labor force and use of child care. The family therapy literature alerts us to problems resulting from family members' tendencies to maintain norms by punishing or withdrawing support for members who attempt to make their own rules. Families who place a great value on closeness tend to place restrictions on the degree of autonomy family members are permitted to exercise in decision making involving their lives. And because women tend to have less power in making autonomous decisions, they are particularly restricted.

Mothers who are the first in the family to send their children to day care outside the home are establishing a new pattern of parent-child interaction. For the single mother, guilt maneuvers designed to ensure conformity with extended family norms are particularly problematic, because she is likely to be loaded already with negative feelings internalized from external attitudes toward single motherhood.

Pressures to conform to an idealized motherhood category by parents who grew up in the 1950s era of the traditional family can be a source of conflict between the two generations. Extended family members may view the single parent as being in a holding pattern. Conformity pressures may center on finding a new mate, thereby repairing the incomplete system at any cost. Even though the rate of remarriage for single mothers has fallen drastically in the past 15 years, and only about half of divorced women remarry, the universal assumption seems to be that women who are alone are in some sort of transitional life stage (Rothblum & Franks, 1987).

Such sources of conflict serve to limit utilization of available support, ranging from respite child care to economic resources. The cost of support may entail grandparents' usurping parental authority over the grandchildren in order to ensure that proper and traditional child-rearing methods be maintained across generational boundaries. Identification of such conflicts and the ventilation of anger and resentments associated with conformity constitute a first step toward successful mediation across generations. Interventions aimed at affirmation of the single-parent family as a whole and complete unit can help extended family members accept that connectedness across generations also requires a degree of autonomy.

SHARING STORIES DESIGNED TO ENFORCE CONFORMITY TO TRADITIONAL GENDER ROLES

Self-help groups or individual interventions can be helpful for finding ways to strengthen family support systems. Demystification and confrontation of powerful intergenerational norms that keep males and females in rigid roles that do not make sense in today's society can perhaps best be accomplished in peer groups. Such exercises can begin with the classic conformity tale of the mother who routinely cut off both ends of a ham before roasting it. Questioned by her daughter about why she did this, the woman replied that it was the way *her* mother always prepared ham. When the daughter then asked her grandmother about the procedure, she discovered that the grandmother always cut the ham because it was the only way she could fit it into her small roasting pan. Group members can be encouraged to share their own experiences of how conformity to a norm valued by the extended family no longer fits the reality of the single-parent family.

The support group provides an excellent forum for sharing of stories that reflect the powerful influence of intergenerational family norms. Because the traditional family is still upheld, even by some well-intended practitioners, as the ideal image against which diverse systems are seen as deviant, group norms that value various family forms can be immensely healing to mothers as heads of households. This normalization process helps move the family forward in its capacity to respond to new realities and demands of single parenting. Intergenerational family norms are, for example, not always encouraging of women's dual roles as competent wage earners and caregivers.

In cases where generational differences in family structure exist and less-than-functional norms are being pressed on the single-parent system, the practitioner can encourage the use of metaphors to identify areas of conflict. Telling stories reflecting how metaphors are used in the family of origin to ensure conformity to family norms can be helpful for the single parent who is having difficulties firming boundaries between her own family and her family of origin. These metaphors can be integrated into the assessment of family support networks, themes, beliefs, and obstacles to support utilization.

One client related the story of how she learned that a "woman's place is in the home." She recalled that her mother had always talked rather wistfully of finding a job outside the home, "one day when you kids are old enough to care for yourselves." Her parents had a very traditional marriage, and her father never took her mother seriously about the job-finding wish. In fact, he often found ways to "put her down" when she spoke of work outside the home. When, at age 45, her mother actually applied for a job as a salesclerk in a local department store, the father began to joke unmercifully about how shy she had always been and her difficulty with math. He even enlisted the support of the client and her three siblings in this "kidding" process. They would all laugh at the image of their mother forcing herself to talk with customers and making mistakes in writing up charges. Her mother, in the end, gave up her dream, withdrew her application, and returned to the home.

It was only later that the client realized the cruelty in this process and the messages about conformity to women's prescribed roles. In her adult years, in therapy, she began to understand the image of her father as the powerful, controlling male. It was he who had the power to influence with language, and it was his story that was to be heard. The lesson was that women's aspirations outside the home were not to be taken seriously. The price to be paid for nonconformity was to be the butt of severe ridicule. These kinds of messages had made it difficult for the client, who had herself entered into a traditional marriage that ultimately failed. As a single parent, she continued to experience difficulties as she found it necessary to move into the work world. She continued to feel that "something was not right" if she was not dependent on a male who would run the family while she took care of children, relationships, and the housework.

Her father's disapproval of this woman's single-parent status and her mother's impotence in the family leadership role had led to a severe rift in her relationships with her extended family. She blamed her mother for failure to serve as a strong role model who could provide support for her daughter in her struggle to become a competent caregiver and wage earner. As the client began to understand the patriarchal family dynamics that prescribe narrow roles for women, she ceased blaming her mother and accepted that the extended family was able to provide task support and limited financial resources when needed. Validation and emotional support, however, were best obtained from extrafamilial support systems.

OVERUTILIZATION OF EXTENDED FAMILY SUPPORT

Increased labor force participation among women in the past few decades has created a trend whereby not only mothers but grandmothers are employed outside the home. Grandparental support usually means that support is provided by grandmothers, especially in the areas of task and emotional support, the traditional realm of women caregivers. Anecdotal evidence in practice indicates that grandmothers often do feel overextended and underappreciated in their roles as prime supporters of their daughters' single-parent families. This is especially true when the grandmother is employed outside the home and in cases where she has more than one offspring who regularly solicit her help for child care and/or financial assistance.

The gender-sensitive practitioner is particularly sensitive to women's overextension in their caregiving role. Network intervention involves reducing solicitations for network support by finding alternative ways to meet needs, maximizing the capacity of the single parent to meet her own needs, showing appreciation, and reciprocating support. At times, grandmothers need to be given permission to limit respite baby-sitting assistance and other task support without feeling guilty.

Grandfathers can perhaps be better utilized as respite caregivers who are capable of and enjoy taking care of their grandchildren. Radin, Oyserman, and Benn (1991) have found that when grandfathers provide a great deal of nurturance for grandchildren, adolescent mothers are more nurturant toward their children and the children tend to be more compliant. Grandfathers not only help provide role modeling for nurturant behavior but also tend to be more playful with children than are grandmothers, who are often preoccupied with taking care of the children's basic needs.

INTRAFAMILIAL SUPPORT:
CHILDREN AS SOURCES OF SUPPORT

Despite the stress associated with the dual roles of parent and wage earner, children do provide emotional support, particularly during the early stages of the family life cycle. Support functions tend to become unidirectional when children reach adolescence; teenagers often cease to provide validation support by way of words of appreciation or engaging in affectionate embrace with their parents. The individuation phase usually means that adolescents wish to separate from the parent while expecting her to be there when needed.

At a time when mother begins to look forward to some independence for herself to pursue interests and activities she has postponed for decades, she may find herself still busy performing chauffeuring and other support functions for her adolescents while getting little in return but indifference and even hostility. Reciprocal emotional support and children's cooperative and compliant behavior may now be replaced with the teenager's frequent criticism and mother blaming. While this type of reduction of rapport and loss of support is similar to what mothers in two-parent households experience, the single parent often does not have a partner to call on for needed support. She may have been so involved in providing for her children's needs as to forfeit social contacts.

In these cases, the practitioner needs to help the single mother establish social networks that often involve extrafamilial support systems. Mothers who have immersed themselves in the parental role sometimes find it difficult to begin preparation for a child-free life. They may even fail to disengage from the mothering role and attempt to keep the adolescent from venturing out of the nest. Conflicts about curfews, dating, and staying on the phone too long may reflect problems of separation.

MALE PARTNERS' RELATIONSHIPS
WITH THE CHILDREN

A male partner can be viewed as a part of the single-parent system or as extrafamilial support, depending on the closeness of the relationship with the mother. If the relationship develops to resemble more of a reconstituted or blended family system, increased potential for support can be expected. (It should be noted that many individuals object to the use of the term *reconstituted* and some do not like the concept of *blended families* or *stepfamilies.* The term *remarried families* seems to be preferred in the current literature, but is not applicable to couples who are cohabiting. Whatever term is used, the process of developing relationships with a new partner presents a major challenge for custodial parents in general.)

The custodial mother is neither married nor single in the traditional sense. The single-parent system in general "comes as a package," and as the mother strives to fit her boyfriend, more or less successfully, into the existing family, older children especially tend to view this change as an intrusion. Such resentments and manifestations of jealousy are common and can lead to children's sabotaging their mothers' relationships, particularly if "reconstitution" comes too rapidly and the children have not had a chance to adjust to the initial change to a single-parent family.

The fact that adolescents are struggling with their own sexuality is compounded by the tendency among children not to view their mothers as individuals with their own needs, but rather as need-meeting agents. Mothers should be encouraged to talk to their children about their own individuation needs and to prepare them for important changes associated with new relationships. Issues that need to be addressed include how close the relationships are likely to become, sexual relationships in the home, and level of authority the male partner will have over the children.

Even under the best of circumstances, conflicts tend to arise during the transitional phase following divorce when a new male partner becomes a part of the family system. Children need to be supported in their opposition to dealing with a new authority figure and their discomfort with having mother take on new lover(s). The practitioner whose belief system is against extramarital sexual relationships must confront the dilemma between his or her own conservative values and the reality of how members of diverse family systems cope with their needs.

MALE PARTNERS AND SUPPORT NEEDS

Sequential relationships can be expected to create more turbulent interactional patterns within the family than is the case with long-term relationships. Supportive, stable relationships are not easily established, however. The single mother must cope with prevalent social stereotypes about divorced women and their sexual needs. These stereotypes can result in sexual harassment on the job and from married male friends and neighbors. These types of encounters tend to make single mothers feel exploited and cautious about developing relationships with males. As these mothers adjust to their single-parent status and become increasingly self-reliant, they become less willing to play the games of submission that tend to be part of male-female relationships. Some men tend to feel threatened by women who demonstrate independence and competence (Arendell, 1986).

Learning to date again is often difficult for single mothers, who may feel like adolescents in a high school popularity contest (Arendell, 1986). New and workable patterns for interpersonal interactions with the opposite sex are not easily established. Support from similar peers can be helpful for those working through the issues of developing supportive relationships with male partners and coping with children's resentment of these new relationships.

There is a great deal of ambivalence among single mothers surrounding the choice of remaining alone or seeking a partnership with a male. This issue is related to support needs, because the options of trying to find male partners or not are more open when mothers can perceive that support can come from various sources. Female friends, neighbors, activities, and peer groups can be viewed as sources of support. Mothers who desperately cling to the idea that support can be found only in male relationships limit some of their options for support. Further, as they grow older their chances of finding suitable partners diminish. First, there is the demographic bind resulting from the scarcity of available men. Single women over 40 outnumber single men at the rate of two to one (Weinberg, Swensson, & Hammersmith, 1983). If a single mother opts to seek a supportive relationship with a male partner, the question of how close that relationship can be without some degree of sacrifice of her independence becomes an issue.

Many single women in general do not wish to marry. Richardson (1986) found that single women, especially those in high-paying occupations, tend to perceive marriage as a drain on time and energy. Women in Richardson's study tended to report more longing for the nurturant aspect of intimate relationships than for sex. Touch deprivation and "skin hunger" are prevalent among single and celibate women, who report intense wishes to be held and a tendency to respond more positively than men to nurturant types of touch (Ainsworth, 1984; Stier & Hall, 1984). The nurturant (communicating acceptance and care) and cathartic (release of suppressed emotions) types of touches have been found to be particularly important aspects of interventions in cases where contact comfort and attachment were found to be lacking (Edwards, 1984).

Holistic network assessment includes determination of the extent to which the need for hugs and nurturant touch is not being met, either by partners or by friend support networks. Network interventions then must seek ways a single mother can meet her needs, either through partnership or friendship networks.

SUPPORT SYSTEMS
AND SAME-SEX PARTNERS

In the process of assessing various sources of support, including support from partners, practitioners must be sensitive to the fact that some mothers have same-sex rather than male partners. Families headed by lesbian mothers are not few in number. There are approximately 2 million lesbian mothers in the United States, and 1.5 million children live in families with lesbian mothers (Hanscombe & Forster, 1981; McGuire & Alexander, 1985). Practitioners who have successfully worked through any biases and homophobic tendencies they may have harbored may still lack information about the special needs of these families. At times, it is best for the practitioner to acknowledge this to the family in order to facilitate the sharing of information.

In working with single mothers who are lesbians, the gender-sensitive practitioner must be careful to inquire about *partnerships* rather than male relationships. Many of the struggles the single parent faces are exacerbated in cases where the executive system is attracted to same-sex partners. Societal stigma and the necessary peer support to counter such stigma are likely to be even more difficult to find for lesbian mothers than for single mothers in general.

DiLapi (1989) suggests that societal values place motherhood on a three-tier hierarchy, with lesbian mothers at the bottom, as the least appropriate to bear and raise children. The marginally appropriate single mother, teen mother, and foster mother comprise the middle of the hierarchy, with the heterosexual married mother at the top, as the most desirable type of motherhood. This stratification results in lack of health care and other support services for families headed by lesbian mothers.

Some lesbian mothers do not find other single parents, or lesbian women who do not parent, very supportive (Chesler, 1986). The reference group of similar peers is likely to be most helpful in providing needed support, and this group is composed of other lesbian single parents. Ponse (1979) explains how members of the lesbian community, as in other communities, seek like persons, partly because individual sexual orientation is protected when it is too risky to reveal such identity.

Although the number of lesbian custodial parents is increasing, many lesbian mothers lose custody battles and are ostracized by their own families when their sexual orientation is revealed. These mothers may be torn between the need for the community and safety of a lesbian support network and the need to seek community with other single parents. Limited family support, court battles to obtain custody of the children, and difficult relationships with estranged spouses make peer and community support essential. Same-sex sexual preference tends to be regarded, even by the court system, as infectious disease, more damaging to children than a father's alcoholism and violent behavior in the home (Chesler, 1986).

The issue of the best interests of the child is primary in custody decisions. Homosexual parents in general are thought to contribute to their children's sexual confusion. Although very few studies have assessed the effect of parental sexual preference on children, common misconceptions about developmental concerns, sexual abuse, and negative peer pressure have not been borne out by research (Cramer, 1986). Of 21 adolescent children of homosexuals studied by Cramer (1986), 3 reported being teased by peers about their parents' sexual preference. Referrals to nationally organized groups such as the Parents and Friends of Lesbians and Gays can be helpful in dealing with negative responses from peers and the other parent. This organization services the needs of individuals with gay-related family problems and offers emotional support and educational resources for obtaining legal advice, child-rearing help, and so forth. Not only custody decisions, but visitation rights are often difficult to negotiate for the lesbian mother who is rejected by her estranged spouse and children.

Single-parent support groups must confront their own biases in working toward the goal of normalization of diverse families that are headed by lesbian and gay parents. The attainment of this goal is likely to be even more challenging than is the self-acceptance process of the single-parent system in general. This can result in a very small peer system and a threat of social isolation.

Integration of isolated lesbian mothers into the mainstream of singles is being achieved by some religious organizations who have developed social activities for lesbians and "straights." Intervention strategies must center on exploring alternative sources of support that can help normalize and legitimate families headed by same-sex partners as one of many diverse family forms.

Chapter 6

EXTRAFAMILIAL SUPPORT

"Nothing could be more commonplace than the widely held assumption that relationships are good for people; nothing could be more startling than the accumulating clinical and epidemiological findings that confirm this view" (Karpel, 1986, p. 17). As Karpel (1986) concludes after a review of the growing body of research on social support, there is a "significant correlation between the presence of supportive relationships in a person's life and his/her physical and psychological health" (p. 17).

This is a chapter about connecting. Feminist family therapists make the point that connection and autonomy are equally to be sought (Goodrich et al., 1988). There is a strongly held belief that people are most likely to thrive in the context of a web of supportive relationships. Women, more than men, are socialized to "know" and to be relationship oriented. Even so, mothers who head families may struggle to build the kind of connections sorely needed by family members. This chapter expands the ecological theme begun in Chapter 4, but focuses on extrafamilial social supports rather on the more material needs of the single-parent family.

For a variety of reasons, mother-headed families are at risk when it comes to obtaining adequate social supports. Many times the needs of the mother are not even recognized, because the needs of the children take priority. It is not unusual even for a helping professional to overlook the mother's needs as he or she focuses upon helping children in the family. As Hicks and Anderson (1989) observe:

Single mothers, more than other groups of unmarried women, may need help in developing a beneficial social support network. Because they have to provide for their children both financially and emotionally, they have difficulty finding the time or energy to survive, much less to address their own needs or go to therapy to make things better. (p. 326)

Certainly, the extended family can be a major resource for a mother-headed family. Establishing supportive ties within the extended family has been treated at length in Chapter 5. In this chapter, we concentrate on building that part of the social network that has to do with friends, supportive groups, and community organizations and services.

SOCIAL SUPPORT
AND THE MOTHER-HEADED FAMILY

Almost everyone can identify a transactional network of relatives, friends, neighbors, coworkers, colleagues, and others. It has been estimated that the average personal network of an adult includes 3 to 6 intimates plus 25 to 40 others (Erickson, 1984). One of the difficulties for single mothers is that the demands of providing for the family both materially and emotionally often deplete their social support system. They often suffer from what has been called a "truncated network" (Erickson, 1984). Divorce, for example, can seriously disrupt the social network of friends and family usually available, especially when the divorce is contentious. The newly divorced single mother and her family can find themselves socially isolated, which can compound their stress. Lack of time and energy often preclude their reaching out for new supportive relations or for repairing old ones. Thus the social support system is further eroded.

A social network in and of itself is not necessarily a support network. Some relationships can be problematic. Often, one of the tasks of the practitioner is to assist in converting such connections into active supports. Social support is experienced when relationships contain positive emotional bonds and when there is the possibility of some needed material assistance. In addition, social support can take the form of needed information or personal feedback.

Clinicians are accustomed to hearing single mothers speak of their longing for other adults as friends "just to talk to." Sometimes they talk of the need to exchange ideas and experiences about parenting. They often voice the wish for someone "to go someplace with" or to share a cup of coffee. In addition to companionship, they express the desire to know other parents who would be willing to exchange child-care responsibilities occasionally. The need for respite from constant focus on care of children is high, especially for those who do not share custody in some way with the other parent.

It seems clear that the functioning of the mother-headed family is greatly affected by the quality of social support available to her and her family. The experience of social isolation can lead to depression, anxiety, and loneliness. As Beal (1980) points out, such isolation on the part of single mothers "tends to intensify the parent-child relationship in such a manner that these women frequently complain of being trapped in a world of children" (p. 257). When she feels she has no place to turn for some relief, the single mother is likely to find that her ability to provide for her children is impaired. When she is unable to negotiate for the kind of social support needed by her family, the children are more at risk, too.

Young children especially are unable to build their own social contacts and may miss some essential ties to the outside world. In addition, children are inclined to take on the concerns and worries of their parents and can get into protective and dysfunctional roles. In effect, a child may try to parent his or her parent. One 5-year-old described such a situation with the poignant remark, "Sometimes my Mom is so sad, I have to write her love letters."

Effective social networks supply the single-parent family with the resource of flexibility it often lacks. Erickson (1975) speaks of the network as a "storehouse of resources" (p. 489). Within that storehouse are problem-solving options, services, valuable information, emotional support, and material assistance. These can provide the single mother with options, and thus flexibility and hope.

PROBLEMS IN BUILDING
SOCIAL SUPPORT NETWORKS

"Although one of the functions of a family is to maintain social and family relationships with members outside the nuclear family, single parents frequently find themselves cut off from extended family and social networks" (Beal, 1980, p. 257). Success in building and maintaining supportive relationships with the world outside the mother-headed nuclear family unit varies with the circumstances of each family. This is a heterogeneous group, as we have noted previously. The majority of such families were created by divorce, but others are in the single-parent category by virtue of a woman's decision not to marry. Some women may have found themselves pregnant and with no opportunity to marry the father, as in the case of many adolescent single mothers. Some families are headed by single mothers due to loss of the fathers through death.

Availability, amount, and quality of social support can be related to circumstances of becoming a single-parent family. While divorce may disrupt the existing network of friends and family, death of a parent can often pull this network closer together, at least initially. Family and friends may gather to support the grieving family and as a way of dealing with their own grief. The woman who chooses to establish a single-parent family may have a well-developed support network that has participated in her decision to bear or to adopt a child. The young unmarried parent who did not have the marriage option may or may not be surrounded by supportive family and friends. Careful assessment must take into account how the circumstances of single parenthood have affected the support system available.

Since most mother-headed families come into existence through separation and divorce, there is need to attend to some special aspects of this group. It is not unusual for a divorced single mother to have the normal connections to her husband's family cut off, or at least to have tension around continuing them. Sometimes this stress in relationships carries over to her children, and positive relationships between children and grandparents suffer.

Predivorce relationships with family and friends may be an important factor in these situations, of course. Very often it is the woman who has been the social ambassador for the couple. Stereotypically, it is the wife who nurtures contacts with friends and even with the husband's own family. Depending upon the circumstances of the divorce, it may prove easier for the woman to maintain connections than for her husband. Unfortunately, it is often the case that there tends to be a break in the relationship with those who were friends of the divorcing couple. People do not want to appear to take sides, for example. Then, too, it sometimes happens that the marital strife that preceded divorce has resulted in less social contact, which is difficult to reestablish after the divorce. Single mothers may also find that their married friends cannot fully invest in a reciprocal relationship (Hicks & Anderson, 1989, p. 328). Married friends may not place the same high priority upon the relationship because of involvement within their own families. In these situations, the practitioner needs to help the single mother to develop more diversity in her support network.

When a woman is employed or has a career, coworkers can be an important avenue for social support. Sometimes, however, these normally positive relationships may have been damaged during the course of a stressful divorce. The emotional drain can leave a woman with little energy for the social activities she ordinarily cherishes. If a woman has not been working outside the home prior to becoming a single mother or has been only minimally employed, opportunity for rewarding relationships with work colleagues does not exist, but may become a focus for building the network in the future.

Even though the circumstances and the quality of social support may vary with the circumstances of becoming a single parent, these families have a great deal in common when it comes to finding needed supports. All face a life transition filled with some uncertainties and difficult developmental tasks. Building, rebuilding, and maintaining social supports for the family are some of the most difficult. Social networks are dynamic and change over time, just as circumstances of the family change. Perhaps what is most important is for the family to develop the skills and processes required to connect in a supportive way with a network.

Some of the components in network building are relationship skills, emotional energy, available time, a pool of contacts upon which to build, and motivation. Obviously, these will differ with the family and its members. Some will have one or two components but lack the others. Some women feel inexperienced and socially inept. They have never had many contacts and do not know where to start.

Probably most single mothers will feel stressed in terms of time, and that must be taken as a realistic concern in network building. Even women who are successful in the world of work outside the home can be vulnerable in this respect. They may possess all the relationship skills necessary, but time pressures block their efforts, sometimes their desires, to take on new relationships and commitments. As one woman said, "I want to meet other adults. I know I need some outlets but with the kids and my work, I sometimes feel relationships would just be a burden—something more to make time for." It is not unusual to hear single mothers talk of having to force themselves to go out to meetings and social gatherings after dealing with their daily responsibilities at work and at home.

Motivation for building a support network is of real concern for many single mothers. A vicious cycle may have been established that is hard to counteract. Lacking the support needed, the single mother may feel increasingly overwhelmed. She begins to feel hopeless about being able to change things and is unable to act, which, of course, distances her even more from sources of support. This, in turn, recycles and increases her negative responses.

Belief systems are a great determinant of whether the single mother is able to act to build the needed network for herself and her family. She may be imbued with the notion that families should be able to take care of themselves without relying on "outsiders." She may have a sense of failure about divorce that would be compounded if others knew she needed personal and parenting help. She may begin to question whether she has failed as a parent.

Some women find it extremely difficult to share their lives and their stories with people outside the family. Family lore often includes an exaggerated sense of privacy, so that it is not correct to talk of one's difficulties with those beyond the family boundary. The helping practitioner should be sensitive to beliefs that militate against the family's connecting with supports. The single mother can frequently be helped to examine and reframe harmful beliefs. This process may require deconstruction of "the family as an island" belief and construction of the positive aspects of support.

Building a social network and participating in it requires emotional energy. The unrelenting nature of the demands of child care and of work certainly takes a toll on the energy level of the single mother. An important and sometimes overlooked factor is the unresolved feeling of loss associated with the circumstances surrounding becoming a single parent. A woman can be legally but not yet emotionally divorced from her former spouse. In the case of death of a spouse, grief may not have been managed well. There can be unanticipated losses associated with the decision to parent alone. For example, an unmarried professional woman who had adopted a child spoke of the loss she felt about having to put some of her former career goals on hold to care for her child. Her joy about having a child initially crowded out such thoughts. The ensuing guilt that accompanied these unanticipated thoughts prompted her to devote every spare moment to child care. There was little room left for supportive relationships with other adults. The sensitive practitioner can facilitate recognition of these unresolved areas of loss and the cost in terms of emotional drain. "Getting on with life" by connecting with adequate social supports may depend upon resolution of loss.

The pool of contacts or the network from which to draw social support varies a great deal with the individual situation. Opportunity for social support is surely linked to this pool, however. One factor to be aware of is how much the pool shrinks when a family goes from two-parent to single-parent status. As suggested previously, divorce especially can diminish the pool or network. Another significant factor with respect to the size of the pool may lie in the mobility of mother-headed families. Masnick and Bane (1980, p. 108) report high levels of residential mobility in the first few years following separation or divorce. Many single parents move several times in the course of two or three years. Each neighborhood differs in the number of opportunities available for social support. Members of a mother-headed family may experience increased feelings of "differentness" in neighborhoods characterized by two-parent families. Opportunities for supportive relationships are also affected by the number and ages of other children in the vicinity.

When the support system is repeatedly disrupted by moves, the family must constantly deal with losses and with rebuilding supports. An example of the results of frequent moves is contained in the experience of a single mother who was forced to move herself and her 8-year-old son three times in two years. Each move carried with it a new job, new school district, and, of course, new neighbors. Both mother and son felt increasing social isolation. The only constant support in their lives came from distant grandparents and one or two friends who were not seen consistently. The child, as might be expected, found it difficult to deal with new teachers and new classmates. He began to express feelings of fearfulness about going outdoors, believing other children did not like him. Feeling sad about friends he had left behind with other moves, he hesitated to make new attachments. As he put it, "I don't want to have anyone else to miss."

A reservoir of connecting skills is crucial to a single mother who must move her family. It is not easy to get acquainted in a new community, especially when you feel different from other families and overwhelmed with responsibility at the same time. A single mother must have the ability to gather information about schools, churches, and recreation facilities. She must know how to make her needs known and how to reach out to connect with those who can help. The tasks for the practitioner are to understand the capacity of the individual mother, to identify the supports needed in new situations, and to promote a sense of competence in resource building.

ASSESSING THE SOCIAL NETWORK

An assessment of the total network is indicated when preparing for the task of building or rebuilding supportive networks in mother-headed families. The ecomap, discussed in Chapter 4, is a useful tool in beginning this process. It can serve as a guide for drawing up a list of significant people in the social network.

Carolyn Atteneave (1980), a proponent of network therapy, suggests ordering network relationships according to degrees of intimacy and emotional significance. She directs clients to construct four lists:

1. people in the immediate household
2. those who are emotionally significant
3. casual acquaintances and functionally related persons
4. persons geographically distant or seldom seen

These can be arranged on a "network map" in a visual representation of the various layers in relationship to one another. The geographical location of each person is important to note, since it may indicate availability of support.

The layers of the network tend to have typical configurations. Generally, the closest layer includes extended family members and good friends. Next may come neighbors and coworkers. Then there will be a group of more peripheral people, of varying levels of significance to family members. These may include teachers, coaches, ministers, doctors, and perhaps various helping professionals. Ministers can be extremely important support figures for some mother-headed families, depending upon the cultural background. Boyd-Franklin (1989) talks of the concept of the "church family" as it relates to black families. She points out, "The minister is usually a central figure in the life of the family and may be sought out by family members for pastoral counselling in times of trouble, pain, or loss" (p. 82).

When completing the lists of relationships, it is important to bear in mind that both positive and negative relationships should be listed. The negative ones may eventually be converted into supportive ones, or

work may need to be done to mediate the effects upon the family. Atteneave rightly cautions, too, that network mapping should be done in the
presence of the therapist, because intense emotions can be generated
that the family may need to process. This is also an opportunity for the
therapist to learn much about the family.

Having elicited the cast of characters in the network, the next task is
to ascertain which of these connections is perceived of as supportive and
how. Questions suggested to guide this inquiry include the following:

1. Of those listed, who is most available? Who is next, and so on, until the
   least available?
2. Of those listed, who would you prefer to be available for support?
3. To whom are you most likely to turn for emotional support (sharing a concern, an important event), for services (child care, transportation, playmates for children), for material aid (money or needed clothing), and/or
   for feedback (checking out a decision, advice, or opinions)?
4. Who do you think you can really count on, even though they may be geographically distant?
5. To whom do you think you give support? What kind? How does it affect
   your life to give such support?

When the list contains people identified as significant but nonsuppor-
tive and/or conflictual, these questions are suggested:

1. Of those identified as not being close or supportive, with whom would you
   like to have a better relationship?
2. Who are the people on the list with whom you once had more supportive
   relationships? How do you explain the change?
3. How would your life be affected if these relationships could be improved?
4. Is there anyone with whom you have a negative relationship but to whom
   you are expected to give support? How does this affect your life?
5. What ideas do any family members have for changing these relationships
   to more favorable ones?

This kind of information will often help the client to begin to consider
other options for developing support. In a sense, the suggestion for the
possibility of a different quality of relationship is embedded in the question. The answers will most certainly serve to guide the practitioner to
potential alternative sources of support to be developed.

Another part of the analysis includes an evaluation not just of the support already available and support needed but some notion of reciprocity. Support does not flow just one way into the mother-headed family. Implicit in the notion of connecting is the idea of interdependence, which carries with it the expectation of exchange of services.

Maintaining reciprocity, a balance between the energy expended and the support obtained, is crucial to the well-being of the mother-headed family. Some mothers who head families can be in situations in which they are giving more to the people in the network than they are receiving. Some may have caretaking roles in the family of origin or with others. This may be particularly true in relation to the extended family. Extended family members can offer valuable aid to the single mother. When such aid is forthcoming, it can alleviate much debilitating stress. This kind of imbalance needs to be addressed in therapy.

Boyd-Franklin (1989) highlights this issue in her writing about black single mothers. It seems true as well for all mothers who head families. When imbalance is found to exist, the task of the therapist with a broader systems perspective is to help the family or the individual parent to balance the scales. This might involve renegotiating relationships in the extended family and/or helping to find other sources of support (p. 204). Some women find they must replace a severely disengaged or nonexistent family of origin with a "friendship family."

The network assessment process provides the practitioner with the opportunity to evaluate the impact of single motherhood upon the family. Some of the network ties will predate the event of becoming a mother-headed family, while some connections will have developed since. It is a useful part of the analysis to consider the perceived balance of losses and gains in support as a result of the change in family form. In some cases it comes as a pleasant surprise for the family to recognize their gains. One single mother who had adopted a child from another country had found an unusually supportive tie with a group of families who had adopted children from the same area.

The network assessment provides a useful guide for change to both the family and the practitioner. In keeping with our feminist-based partnership approach, family members are encouraged to participate in identifying what changes are needed and desired. Having completed the assessment, the family and practitioner are prepared to design ways to build and/or rebuild the support system.

HELPING TO BUILD
SOCIAL SUPPORT NETWORKS

Nancy R. was the single parent of 4-year-old Sam. Nancy had never been married, lived alone with Sam, and was studying to become a legal secretary. Her only income was from AFDC, although she had managed to obtain a grant and some financial assistance to help with her education. Her adviser at the junior college she attended had referred her for counseling. The presenting complaint was her sense of being overwhelmed with responsibility, loneliness, and possible depression. She was also bothered about her increasing lack of tolerance, sometimes bordering on resentment and anger, with respect to caring for Sam.

In the initial phase of therapy, Ms. R. was involved in completing a genogram and an ecomap. These procedures helped to refine the sources of stress, some potential resources, and goals for change. For example, Ms. R., now 23 years old, was alienated from her family of origin at the time of her pregnancy with Sam. Her parents had favored abortion, which Ms. R. adamantly rejected. The estrangement had persisted until the past year, when her parents had softened and begun to take an interest in her and her child. Much of the anger between them had been resolved, and Ms. R. now counted them as a dependable resource in her life. Even so, she was aware of feeling socially isolated.

Early discussions with Ms. R. revealed that Sam's father was not currently in the picture, having moved to another state. He had not proved supportive during the pregnancy and seemed to have little interest in his son. While Ms. R. had strong ties to extended family, there were few other social supports. She was lonely but had few social skills and felt guilty about leaving Sam other than to attend classes. She felt depressed and powerless much of the time, felt ashamed of her circumstances, and seemed badly in need of external supports.

The meaning of single parenting for Ms. R. had clearly been associated with separation from significant people in her family, but it had also distanced her from friends. During the course of her pregnancy, she was cut off from most of her school friends. In her four years of parenthood, she had not made new friends. She had been out on one or two dates, but again felt that she owed it to Sam to be with him whenever she was not in classes or studying. She had no one to call upon for babysitting except her parents. Her mother cared for Sam while she attended school, and, not wanting to be too dependent upon her parents, she hesitated to ask for more respite child-care support from them.

ESTABLISHING THE NEED FOR SUPPORT

Building a support network seemed essential for Ms. R., although she was not immediately aware of that fact. Many women who head families do not automatically associate their feelings of stress and depression with lack of social support. In a sense, what may be needed in the beginning is an educational approach, so that this connection can be made clear. Making such a link helps to normalize the stress, which in and of itself can alleviate some of the problematic feelings. With Ms. R., the task was complicated by her attitude that it was wrong for her to need outside support. When the therapist pointed to her isolation as a key element in her feelings of depression and being overwhelmed, Ms. R. would make such comments as: "I got myself into this. I have only myself to blame and it was my decision to keep the baby. I can't expect others to burden themselves for me now."

Building a support network with her began with changing the belief system that precluded her asking for and accepting needed help. Ventilating feelings of guilt about having violated her parents' expectations was a prerequisite of her developing a more acceptable vision of herself and her behavior. This took some time and, in part, involved going over the story of her pregnancy and putting it into the context of her life at that time. She began to accept that she had not only a need but a right to have support in her life and to think of her own needs.

Another chink in this rigid belief system was accomplished by appealing to a major strength—her interest in being an effective parent. Caring for herself was tied directly to her ability to function well as a parent. She became more accepting and more cognizant of the goal of building outside support as she realized the benefits not only for her but also for Sam. If she were relieved of stress, she would be much better able to meet Sam's needs. In addition, Sam's need for playmates and contact with a variety of adults was apparent. Once she had gotten over that hurdle, the connecting work could begin.

Individual counseling sessions with Ms. R. supported the connecting work by focusing on the resolution of her sense of loss from the past and her fears about the future. She was able to see how her conflict in these areas was an obstacle to her being able to establish the supportive and meaningful relationships she desired. With some of the emotional work done in preparation, Ms. R. was ready for the task of connecting.

BUILDING THE SOCIAL SUPPORT SYSTEM

As Ms. R. gained understanding and acceptance about her need for support, her motivation for developing such contacts increased. A survey of her existing network was completed. This included people of varying degrees of frequency of contact as well as significant people from her past with whom she had lost contact. She was encouraged to reach out to friends from high school, many of whom were still in the area. She was successful in reestablishing one or two contacts that she found quite rewarding. One woman was also a single parent who was delighted to have someone with whom to exchange experiences. This provided a playmate for Sam, and the two mothers worked out an arrangement to swap baby-sitting services occasionally. Trading services can be a tremendous resource for single parents.

Ms. R. began to feel empowered enough through this success to risk reaching out to potential new friends in other settings. She found herself talking to her classmates and joining them for coffee breaks and becoming involved in study groups. She even discovered a support group for single mothers who were students at the school. Her network map included a past connection to a church group. Although she did not care to return to that particular church, she found another that had an active program for young adults. The therapist also helped her to connect to a community agency that specialized in short-term groups for women. She took advantage of a parenting group for single mothers and a "self-esteem" group.

The exposure to others in the groups she had joined helped her to normalize her own experience, which reduced the reactivity about her own situation. She felt greatly empowered as she was able to share her story of single parenting with others. A result of all of this was Ms. R.'s growing sense of confidence as a parent and as a woman. The social support system that had been established opened a much more hopeful path to the future than the one she had envisioned in her isolation.

SELF-HELP GROUPS AND SUPPORT

There is an accumulating body of knowledge about the value of self-help groups in alleviating various types of problems. Certainly, self-help groups can be an enormous resource for single mothers. Such groups proved to be a critical factor in the changes achieved by Ms. R. Fortunately for her, one of the counselors at her junior college had been instrumental in helping some single mothers form a support group. As time went on, Ms. R. found a local Parents Without Partners group of value. Her church provided a self-generated group of women who were helping one another with problems concerning self-esteem.

The effectiveness of self-help groups for single mothers has many facets. The group members share information about coping with ordinary tasks, such as money management and finding day care. Support groups of peers also help in redefining the mother's social and individual self. As she becomes comfortable with meeting new people in the group, she begins to develop a sense of self in relationships with friends as well as with family members. Group members provide support by encouraging a positive perspective on the experiences of single parents. Universalization of the experiences of the "independent" parent is accomplished, along with the identification of common obstacles and opportunities in the everyday lives of one-parent families.

PROFESSIONALLY LED GROUPS

Referrals to professionally led groups are often indicated to help the family adjust, especially during the period shortly after divorce or separation. Groups such as those for children of divorce, the whole family, or adolescent parents have been very successful in teaching coping skills, expanding support networks, and promoting adjustment to changes (Bell, Charping, & Strecker, 1988; Crosbie, Burnett, & Newcomer, 1990; Kissman, 1992). Professionally led groups can be a timely resource for the ongoing development of the single-parent family as it moves beyond those tasks associated with the early stage of its formation. Multiple-family therapy, in which two or more families are brought together around a common issue such as parenting, may be particularly helpful. This type of psychosocial intervention is indicated in cases of disruptive life changes, social isolation, and parenting problems (O'Shea & Phelps, 1985). Groups such as these can serve as vehicles for support and for exchange of ideas and experiences about the challenges of single parenthood.

Single mothers may benefit from professionally led groups that are focused upon entering the job market, economic issues, assertiveness, and network building. Single fathers, for reasons addressed later in the book, may need groups centered upon "fathering," and may have specific questions about child care and relationships (Gordon, 1990a). All of these groups provide the opportunity for enrichment as well, since the participants are likely to compare problems and solutions.

DATING AND SEXUAL RELATIONSHIPS

An important part of building support for the single mother often has to do with the process of developing relationships with men. Sometimes this can present a major challenge. The custodial mother is neither married nor single in the traditional sense. Because the single-parent system in general "comes as a package," the mother strives to fit a new male friend, more or less successfully, into the existing family. One woman client put the issue this way: "I may be interested in a man but that is not enough. I have to watch how he is with my child. He and Tommy have to get along, too." Another woman spoke of how a potential male friend immediately "took over" and started telling her how to discipline her children. His assumption was that they missed the "firm hand of a father."

As Morawetz and Walker (1984) point out, many children resent what they perceive as intrusion into the family by their mothers' male friends. This may be true especially of older children who are accustomed to special roles with their mother. Manifestations of resentment and jealousy are common. Some children, of course, feel very protective of the noncustodial parent and believe it a betrayal if they accept the new man in their mother's life. In any case, the single mother's attempts to establish social and romantic relationships constitute a complicated family matter.

The response of the child to the single mother's interest in male companionship may vary with age. As discussed in Chapter 5, the fact that adolescents are struggling with their own sexuality is compounded by the reality that children do not view their mothers as individuals with their own needs, but rather as need-meeting agents. Mothers should be encouraged to talk to the children about their own individuation needs, including the developing of relationships with male partners. Even under the best of circumstances, however, conflicts tend to arise during the transitional phase when a new man becomes actively engaged as a part of the family system. Such a transition is especially complex when the family is still in the early phase of single parenthood, when the family is struggling with realignment. The practitioner can help the family understand the stress as related to the difficult transitions occurring within the family. During the transition when a male friend is entering the family, children will need to be supported in their anxiety about what they may perceive as a threat to their father's position.

Chapter 7

ETHNIC FAMILIES

The strength of the single-parent family within ethnic communities in the face of poverty and discrimination should not be underestimated. This is particularly true of African-American single-parent families, whose support networks serve as models for family survival strengths. McGoldrick, Anderson, and Walsh (1989) caution against treating African-American mothers as superwomen, however. According to these authors, there is a tendency to minimize some of the issues of concern for African-American women in general. One critical concern is the high female-to-male ratio, which prevents many women from being able to choose to have male partners or including males as part of their support systems.

Demographic data and other information about factors that have impacts on the lives of ethnic single-parent families are important in correcting the myth of matriarchy and other misinformation that blames women for many of the problems attributable to racism, unemployment, and underemployment. Information about cultural variations, however, does not substitute for strong self-awareness about one's own ethnicity and feelings about cultural diversity. A holistic view of the context of ethnic families includes both problems and strengths, such as community resources and religious and family support. The flexible system of exchange and emphasis on collectivity among many ethnic families serve as examples of functional survival strategies for single-parent families in general.

Although feminist-based practice seeks to reduce power hierarchies in human relationships, it has been criticized for ignoring the need for sensitivity to ethnic differences, much as conventional interventions have been lacking in gender sensitivity. Practitioners who are often ill at ease working with clients of different race and ethnicity (Davis & Proctor, 1989) may be more comfortable memorizing lists of ethnic variations than engaging in the difficult task of developing ethnic self-awareness. Although some generalizations about the survival strengths of ethnic families are helpful, such information is not a substitute for confronting one's own ethnocentric bias and remaining open and positive about ethnic differences in our work with clients.

The terms *race* and *ethnicity* are often used interchangeably in the social science literature. We have not attempted to make any distinction here, although color affects the lives of individuals more significantly than do language and culture (Hopps, 1982). Our discussion is generally directed toward both racial and cultural differences. One exception is in the discussion of immigrant families, where the effects of language and culture are particularly strong during the process of assimilation, when family members are negotiating old and new cultural norms.

In this chapter we discuss practitioner self-awareness and sensitivity to ethnic difference reflected by the ability to see problems experienced by ethnic mother-headed families as similar to those of other single-parent families. At the same time, sensitivity to different environmental factors, ranging from interaction with work and school systems to lower wages and greater degree of poverty among ethnic families, is an important part of problem definition.

We discuss the concept of ethclass, or the combined influence of ethnicity and class, in the lives of single-parent families. Throughout our discussion we elaborate on a contextual rather than individual deficit view of family problems. Some of the strengths of ethnic families, such as flexible systems of exchange, extended family, and community support, are stressed.

SENSITIVITY TO ETHNICITY

Practitioners' sensitivity to ethnicity begins with self-awareness about ethnocentrism as a powerful and negative aspect of our everyday lives. We live in a stratified society where individuals are ranked based on gender, ethnicity, and class. Practitioners must acknowledge how discriminatory evaluation of clients' survival strengths and abilities is operative in the human services, which reflect societal negative evaluations of ethnic, class, and cultural differences.

Pinderhughes (1989) views power inequalities between workers and clients of diverse ethnic backgrounds as a major obstacle in professional relationships. She charges practitioners with changing negative cultural identity and enhancing clients' power. This process begins with emphasizing clients' sense of mastery or competence and extends to the capacity to produce desired effects on others.

The practitioner who is sensitive to ethnic issues perceives diversity as functional survival strengths, and this challenge is operative whenever individuals of various cultures, ethnicities, classes, and genders are charged with evaluating one another's competence and ways of living. Ethnically competent practice requires what Devore and Schlesinger (1987) refer to as "layers of understanding" about the interaction of ethnicity and class. This layer of understanding extends one step further when gender is added to class-competent and ethnically competent practice.

For example, women from ethnic groups that are stigmatized are under extreme pressure to adapt to dominant society's conventions (McGoldrick et al., 1989). Even well-intentioned practitioners, in the process of enforcing rules for acceptable behavior, sometimes frame behavior associated with family survival in negative terms. A middle-class worker, for example, was puzzled by a mother's decision to move into a house where all the floor coverings needed to be replaced. The most competent way, in her view, was to have repairs completed prior to the move. However, the family could not afford to pay rent elsewhere during the lengthy process of repairs, since their budget would allow refurbishing only one room at a time.

Consciousness-raising begins with practitioners' confrontation of their own tendency to hold up the "majority" cultural norms as superior to other cultural or ethnic norms. Such ethnocentric views violate social work values of individual dignity and worth and contradict gender-sensitive practice principles of celebrating the diversity of women's experiences. Letting go of the artificial dichotomy of "white versus other" takes a conscientious effort to expand rigid boundaries established when we quantify comparisons across ethnic groups as better than, less than.

The practitioner who is sensitive to ethnicity and class is committed to attending carefully to the client's story. This may require extra restraint of the natural tendency to bring premature closure to the human experience based on one's own culture- or class-centered view. This challenge is often difficult to meet when we formulate hypotheses about what the client's world is like. A worker who asks impoverished family members how they celebrate events and enjoy good times together might choose to ask about time spent with extended family and low-cost community activities. Probing about dining out, shopping, and travel, which the family can ill afford, can create feelings of inadequacy among family members.

Minor variations in the ways questions are asked can set the stage for a more or less egalitarian relationship between worker and client. Asking about how the family has attempted to resolve the presenting problem(s), what worked well and what did not, reflects a positive expectation about the family's ability to explore alternatives. Conversely, asking whether the family has tried a specific approach—for example, "Have you tried to praise Johnny when he is behaving well?" —has a more deficit connotation than, for instance, "What happens when you praise him for his behavior, or catch him when he is good?"

UNDERSTANDING ETHCLASS

Obviously, not all ethnic families are impoverished, but the concept of *ethclass* is important in understanding how ethnicity and class combine to form a hierarchy of oppression that impedes individual quality of life. A contextual view of individual and family problems reveals that for Latina and African-American mother-headed families, the wage structure and resource base is much lower than for their white counterparts. Some 68% of African-American single-parent families, for example, live in poverty, compared with 38% of white single-parent families (Danziger, 1989).

Intervention with impoverished families requires assessment of economic resources. The practitioner serves as a broker, linking the family to existing resources, and as an advocate, mediating between various social agencies and the client and advocating that the client's needs be met adequately and in a timely manner. The gender-sensitive practitioner assesses family problems as being partly "political," or attributable to scarce resource allocation, racial discrimination in wage labor, and mother blaming. Practitioners advocate for affordable and adequate child care and seek to expand community resources that strengthen the capacity of women to be both wage earners and caretakers.

African-American families are twice as likely to be headed by mothers than are their white counterparts (50%, compared with 25% in the population at large), and more than 50% of single-parent families are poor (Kamerman & Kahn, 1989). Practitioners need to be keenly aware of the need for support services, educational and training programs that enable these mothers to enter the labor market at wages that provide at least minimum basic needs.

Recognizing the limitations of past policies and programs aimed at encouraging recipients of Aid to Families with Dependent Children to enter the work force without adequate child-care, transportation, and other support services, the gender-sensitive social work practitioner and policymaker seeks to encourage impoverished mothers to speak out and to identify their needs.

Positive examples of the consequence of active participation of women consumers have surfaced in the past among women welfare recipients who have organized meetings and newsletter publications to identify and publicize their needs (*Hunger Action Forum,* 1990). Other successful community organizations have been formed in some urban housing development projects where property management by parents who are involved in problem assessment has resulted in greatly improved living conditions for these tenants. These types of organizations date back to the 1960s, when impoverished mothers were instrumental in promoting some positive changes in the welfare of their families. One of the major obstacles to further progress for mothers' rights organizations in the past was male leadership that sought welfare benefits but did not listen to mothers' needs for day care and other child welfare services that would allow mothers to work outside the home (West, 1981).

The need for women to be heard and to have a part in defining their own problems is particularly important when class and ethnicity combine to form a hierarchy of inequalities. The high attrition rate for impoverished African-American women in mental health settings is partly attributable to practitioners' proceeding to "solve the problems" without adequately consulting the clients' points of view (Franklin, 1988). The practitioner need not claim expertise in cultural norms among diverse ethnic populations, but should encourage women to name their own experiences and to identify strengths in their daily lives and in their collective network systems.

A case illustration by Lewis and Kissman (1989) exemplifies how careful attention to the presenting problem, as it relates to the context in which the family lives, can lead to joint redefinition of the target problem in work with a woman from a lower-income background. The woman in this case was reluctant to ask her drug-dependent partner to leave their residence, despite his lack of contribution to economic or emotional needs of the family. The practitioner sought clarification: "I hear you saying that you don't want to put him out, but are angry about the way he treats you and the kids. Am I right about this?" The woman nodded. "What is it that he does for you that is more important than the lack of support?" The woman answered, "If he were not there, the neighborhood dope dealers would break into the house and the kids would be in danger." The intervention could then proceed to addressing her target problem of securing a safe environment for her family rather than focusing on her relationship with her partner.

ETHNIC IDENTITIES AND COLLECTIVITY

The sensitive practitioner is aware that cultural and ethnic identities are important aspects of cognitive and coping skills (Granger & Portner, 1985). Ethnic identity affects an individual's sense of competence, responsibility, control, and mutuality (Lum, 1986). In other words, cultural identity influences interpersonal interaction within families and within any social organization.

Women and people of color tend to associate individual competence with the competence of significant others as a group. Mutuality, for example, has to do with mutual responsibility of family members for each other. Individual wishes are subordinated to the goal of the whole family; the interdependence of kinship networks and the community systems as a whole are collective strengths (Lum, 1986).

The practitioner who is well versed in traditional structural family therapy and can identify "functional" generational boundaries needs to modify the normative model to include such cultural diversities as grandmothers' key roles in the rearing of grandchildren. Grandmothers and other members of the extended family often should be included in the family assessment as a legitimate part of the decision-making system rather than as a more distant influence. This type of interdependence should be seen as a family survival strength rather than as dysfunctional interference and enmeshment. Strong interdependence between parents and children in Latino families is also a functional norm based on collective rather than individual survival values (Ho, 1987).

Single-parent families in which children are parented by both mother and grandmother can be referred to as binuclear. A young mother may define her role as coparental in cases where extended family and a strong community support network help in parenting her children. Clarification of the executive system function and strengths becomes more complex as a young single mother matures and becomes more capable of parenting alone. She may need help in claiming her maternal role at the expense of forfeiting some support for autonomy. The skills involved in assessing the benefits and costs of extended family networks apply to utilization of other social networks as well. Lindblad-Goldberg (1987, pp. 39-46) suggests that the practitioner probe the following points in order to assess the functioning and reciprocity of the mother's social network (a minimum criterion for a helpful network is that mother receives at least as much as she gives):

1. what positive, negative, or mixed feelings or thoughts the mother has toward each network person
2. how frequently each network person helps the mother by providing emotional support when she needs it in the areas of parenting, personal relationships, and work stress
3. how frequently each network person helps her by providing assistance when she needs it in the areas of child care, finances, material goods, and household maintenance

In addition to extended family, supportive community networks have been part of important survival strategies in the African-American community, for example. Members of the community who are not related to the family often help provide needed material assistance and help with child rearing. These types of flexible systems of exchange have even involved "informal adoptions," where children have been raised by friends and neighbors.

FLEXIBLE SYSTEMS OF EXCHANGE

Informal systems of exchange are important collective survival strategies in ethnic communities. Assessment tools such as the ecomap tend to become complex as many ethnic families include "fictive kin" or nonblood relatives who have taken in children to raise through informal adoptions or are partly responsible for child rearing of their friends' children (Boyd-Franklin, 1989). Informal adoptions are often seen as preferable to the formal adoption network, through which African-American children may be adopted out to white families.

The National Association of Black Social Workers strongly advocates for same-race adoptions because cross-racial adoption results in a severing of the child's cultural identity. When children are removed from their ethnic environment, they tend to associate their ethnicity negatively, because they are alienated from their culture of origin. Positive role models and orientations about the child's ethnicity may help, but they do not adequately address the loss of being dislodged from the ethnic community.

Other types of in-kind support include absentee parents and paternal family who often help provide needed material and task support to the single mother and her child, even when formal child support payments are not forthcoming (Danziger, 1988). Community support systems within ethnic communities have historically been powerful sources of collective survival strengths for families. The African-American heritage, for example, is characterized by strong religious organizations and mutual aid for survival in the face of discrimination and a hostile environment (McGoldrick, 1982). Flexible systems of exchange reflect creativity and ability on the part of ethnic families in their interaction with the larger environment.

RELIGIOUS SUPPORT SYSTEMS

Practitioners who identify with a strong feminist-based service perspective may be hesitant to include religious organizations as part of a network assessment of support resources for female clients. Such organizations tend to be perceived by feminists as disempowering for women (King, 1989; Sanford & Donovan, 1989). Many women, however, and perhaps especially ethnic women, are able to capitalize on the support and spiritual experience offered by a patriarchal church community.

The practitioner who is sensitive to his or her clients' ethnicity is aware of the strong role of the church in promoting community cohesion among African Americans and Latinas. Church affiliation, as a supportive resource, may therefore become an important part of assessment and intervention, ranging from a source of emotional and spiritual support to social networking. Church leadership in ethnic communities has been instrumental, for example, in mobilizing groups to improve living conditions of impoverished families. Church leaders have also helped to mediate problems between families and schools and other community institutions, and churches have often helped provide emergency assistance—food and other basic needs—for impoverished families.

Many churches have support groups and social activities for single adults that can help single mothers to feel a part of a community. Because social isolation is one of the major problems faced by mothers heading families alone, interventions aimed at creating a sense of belonging in the community are particularly important.

Families vary greatly in their use of support from religious communities. These differences exist between cultural groups as well as within each cultural community. In their interaction with the larger environment, levels of acculturation and assimilation within groups may be as important as differences between cultural groups. This is particularly true for immigrant families, where problems associated with developmental stages of the family are often compounded by cross-generational differences in the old versus new cultural values and norms.

IMMIGRANT FAMILIES

Children in immigrant families are often charged with serving as cultural liaisons, translating language and cultural norms to their parents. Parental competence and authority are sometimes eroded as the child moves into the executive role and becomes overdirective in decision making, ranging from major purchases of goods and services to social activities.

The combination of immigrant and single-parent status may create a special need for the family to rely on the children to share in tasks and decision making. This is especially true where extended family and social support networks are in short supply. Immigrant families who do not reside in large ethnic communities tend to be isolated from social activities and support networks that could buffer the "culture shock" of adjusting to new cultural norms. Referrals to church groups and other community organizations that can offer informational and emotional aid to the family can be helpful.

For second-generation children in immigrant families, the process of conforming to new cultural norms can be all-consuming. Their developmental needs dictate that they align themselves not only with their peer culture, but with the larger culture as well. The individuation phase of the family life cycle can be even more painful when the adolescent feels the need to reject not only parental authority but strong cultural identities as well. Cultural clashes can result when the children no longer wish to speak or to be spoken to in the language of origin, refuse to consume ethnic food, and refuse to socialize with members of their ethnic group. These clashes are particularly severe in ethnic families that do not value adolescents' separation and autonomy to the extent that North Americans do.

In Latino and Asian-American cultures, which frown on divorce and female-headed families even more than the dominant U.S. culture does, family members are struggling to maintain positive self-image and sense of competence against multiple societal forces that predict doom and failure for these family units. Affirmation of the capability of the family to provide nurturance, support, and socialization is a priority intervention strategy, followed by the strengthening of supportive networks and mediation of conflicts within the family. Parental peer support groups can be effective in implementing these interventions, and immigrants from the same culture can address issues associated with cultural rejection. Feelings associated with not belonging or being in the out-group in the community often must be confronted in tandem with the personal rejection many parents feel when their children carve out lives of their own.

When groups of similar ethnic peers are not available, families of diverse ethnic backgrounds can form cohesive units around common issues of dual socialization and assimilation. Individual interventions also should be focused on harmonizing the dual socialization process and assimilation of the family. Lum (1986) explains how the process of assimilation into the new culture must be accomplished with respect for the need to maintain ties to the old culture. This socialization process is dual, in that members are not encouraged to reject but to cherish the best in their culture of origin, which then paves the way for acceptance of some new norms. The practitioner who values cultural diversity can, for instance, reinforce the family's need to speak the language of origin in the home, while exploring the feasibility of the family's taking camping vacations together to explore their new country and to interact with other vacationers.

Pinderhughes (1989) suggests that practitioners can become culture brokers when families are experiencing ambivalence about old and new cultural norms. Mothers can be encouraged to compare their lives in the new and old cultures, to examine the sense of loss they have faced, to determine what is useful in the new culture and what American values they wish to adopt and have their children learn. Conflict arises when first-generation parents are faced with the reality that they have very little to say about their children's adoption of prevalent values, such as individualism, in some North American cultures. The impact of these value changes on family interaction often clashes with parental authority, particularly where that authority is minimized in the new culture.

Chapter 8

ADOLESCENT PARENTS

Adolescent parents constitute a subgroup of single parents who are most likely to be identified as "at risk" for problematic parenting practices, even neglect and abuse (Hawkins & Duncan, 1985; Wise & Grossman, 1980). This negative focus on adolescent parents as a homogeneous group parallels studies that have addressed factors that serve to strengthen parental adjustment and well-being among young mothers (Buchholz & Gol, 1986; Gottlieb, 1985). Interventions aimed at promoting self-help through skills training and strengthening support networks have been effective in preparing young mothers for the parenthood role. Parenting skills training, for example, has been found to enhance young parents' affectionate responding to their children and to promote responsive parental style (Campbell, Lutzker, & Cuvo, 1982).

Parental skills training for adolescent mothers is an essential component of a comprehensive service delivery that also includes transportation, child care, financial assistance, and other services that help young mothers stay in school. School-based teen parent programs are often limited, however, both in duration and in the number of services offered to increase the opportunity for school attendance.

In this chapter, we describe how a collaborative project between a school of social work and a teen parent program helped expand services to include parental skills, knowledge of child development, and support utilization. This group intervention began with mutual peer support to confront feelings about the new and often unintended parental role. The groups then moved on to child development knowledge and parental skills to enhance child-centered attitudes and behaviors. Group members processed information about their expectations of children, ranging from toilet training to obedience of parents' commands. After the intervention, group members scored significantly higher on a scale measuring relatively child-centered parental attitudes.

Strengthening support utilization from extended family and the father of the child involved social skills training, such as knowing when and how to ask for help, as well as raising expectations of the father of the child to be involved in providing material, task, and emotional support for the mother and child. Partner involvement in decisions about second pregnancy prevention was discussed in terms of expanding the options for young mothers to prepare for future roles as wage earners and caregivers.

In addition to parental training, comprehensive services that meet the needs of the adolescent parent and her child include child care, financial assistance, transportation, and housing. These basic needs are very much linked to school retention, because the welfare of the adolescent-parent family is closely linked to the mother's ability to stay in school. A teen mother has only a 50% chance of graduating from high school, and will earn half of what a woman who waits until age 20 to have her first child will earn (Edelman, 1987). Basic needs such as transportation, child care, financial assistance, and employment are met through a combination of informal and formal support networks made up of extended family and community services.

Linkages to community services are particularly important because teen mothers tend not to know about such services and therefore underutilize them (Franklin, 1988). From 25% to 30% of teen mothers cannot live with their own parents or the parents of their children's fathers (Tereszkiewics, 1984), and many need to be referred to local housing authorities and other services to secure basic needs for food, shelter, and day care. A referral to school-based teen parent programs can be the most desirable alternative, because these programs offer many of the services needed for the young mother to stay in school. Teen parent programs usually offer case management services, referrals to community services, and, in some cases, housing, food, and clothing on a temporary basis.

TEEN PARENT PROGRAMS

Teen parent programs offer peer support and a more accepting climate for adolescent parents than is the case in the mainstream public school system. The range of services offered by these programs includes day care, transportation, case management, and other support services essential for the adolescent to stay in school. Teen programs are, however, usually limited in duration to a six-month period and only serve a relatively small proportion of the population in need of services (Roosa, 1986). Further, parental skills training is not always a part of the comprehensive services package offered by school-based and other teen parent programs (Roosa, 1986). Parental training and decision-making skills are needed for successful coping with day-to-day demands associated with the new parental role (Brindis & Jeremy, 1988).

SOCIAL SKILLS TRAINING
TO ENHANCE SUPPORT UTILIZATION

Parental skills training has been shown to be effective in helping adolescent parents cope with their new roles as parents (Lutzker, Wesch, & Rice, 1984; Rosenberg & Repucci, 1985). Adolescent parenthood tends to be stressful because of the multiple demands on the mother in negotiating age-related developmental transformations, completing her education, and taking on a new parental role. The onset of early parenthood often finds the young mother preoccupied with her own developmental needs while lacking requisite parental skills to take care of her child adequately (Thompson, 1986).

Interventions with the adolescent parent are not limited to parental skills training but also include helping her gain confidence in her ability to be a good parent, to resolve conflict between her child's needs and her own needs, and to seek respite care when she needs it. Most new mothers face the challenging task of combining family and work/ student roles, and these decisions require skills or competencies that guide decision making about future life options (Quackenbush, 1987). In the transitional stage of adolescence, young women are making decisions about how to combine occupational and family roles (Buchholz & Gol, 1986). These choices involve whether one can take good care of a baby while holding down a full-time job or going to school full time.

Skills training and knowledge development can influence a young mother's ability to exercise some of her options.

The practitioner must confront his or her own values regarding a young mother's ability to parent. In light of the fact that an estimated 94% of teen mothers opt to keep their babies (Baumrind, 1980), the tasks for the gender-sensitive practitioner are to help the mother gain a sense of control in the difficult interface between work/school and caretaker roles and to help her learn to utilize supportive networks to the maximum extent possible.

An intervention research project involving a collaborative effort by the public school system and a graduate school of social work was conducted by one of the authors to provide parental training for adolescent mothers enrolled in a teen parent program. Early on, it became clear that parental skills training was interrelated with other needs, particularly the need to strengthen support utilization and to help resolve some of the conflicts with extended family. Academic skills training and case management were provided by the school-based teen parent program. Parental skills training was seen by the school administration and staff as complementary to the school's mission, that of enhancing competence of the teen mothers enrolled in the program. Three female graduate students conducted two weekly group sessions with a total of 30 pregnant and parenting teen mothers who were enrolled in the program. The mothers were randomly selected from the school population of 120 students to participate in the two groups. The participants were then given the option of not participating, but all who were selected chose to participate.

The group norms established early in the year granted ownership of the group to the participants; that is, group members were advised that the mission of the group was to strengthen parental skills, but that this was their group and that members' input was essential. Participation was encouraged in developing rules of confidentiality and attendance. Suggestions were solicited for improvement of the group content and process by means of brief written feedback from group members at the end of each session. As a result of this interactive process, group leaders brought snacks for everyone for mid-morning break. This proved helpful in establishing rapport as well as preventing hunger pangs resulting from harried schedules and missed breakfasts. The group attendance rate of 75% was higher than for average school attendance, and more than half of the members participated actively in the group, with one-third rarely participating.

The participants began the 90-minute group sessions by sharing the negative reactions of relatives and neighbors to the adolescents' pregnancies. Before moving on to the mission of strengthening parental skills, these young mothers needed first to ventilate feelings and attend to their own needs for acceptance by the group leaders. Throughout the group sessions, the mothers' support needs became an important part of the group's agenda. Balancing the focus of attention between the mothers' and the children's needs was imperative, because these mothers were very much in need of validation and emotional support. They tended to resent it when they felt that too much attention was being directed away from their needs and toward their babies.

Mutual peer support was an integral part of the group dynamics and was seen as interrelated with the agenda of training in parental skills and coping with everyday demands. Group members provided information and validation support to each other as well as corrective negative feedback when one member, for example, wanted to ruminate about the negative reaction of her extended family to her pregnancy. The group was able to refocus attention on the problem solving needed in the here and now, and to move toward planning for day-to-day needs and activities. The question, What do you need to do now? became an important one as members role-played and rehearsed new responses found to be effective in enhancing their coping skills (Azar & Twentyman, 1986). Not all of the young mothers needed to find new ways to respond to criticism about prematurely becoming parents. Some teens felt that parenting at age 16 was a normative and multigenerational experience that was not necessarily negative.

Problems related to conflicts and barriers to effective support utilization were seen as an integral part of parental coping. Recognizing the need for and planning when and how to ask for help involves skills that the adolescent is in the process of developing (Elkind & Bowen, 1979). Enhancing support utilization involved role-playing assertive interactions; skills in identifying, planning, and asking for what one needs; negotiating exchange of services, such as baby-sitting; resolving conflict by use of "I" messages; and expressing appreciation for support received.

Kissman and Shapiro (1990) describe some examples of how adolescent mothers define their needs for assistance and how this can lead to more sophisticated problem-solving skills in asking for help. The first skill needed is the ability to define problem areas ("I feel as though I never have time for myself anymore"). Second is the capacity to articulate felt needs ("I need to get away for a while and spend time with my friends"). Third is the ability to identify a range of possible solutions and weigh their costs and benefits ("Maybe my baby's paternal grandmother can baby-sit for me for a while"). And fourth is the ability to project possible outcomes into the future ("Then I could get away and I might feel better when I got home"). The skills of showing appreciation for help received and identifying the need to reciprocate help are also important for ensuring ongoing support options.

Other issues related to support utilization involved resolving "executive" power conflicts between teens and their parents. There is an inherent conflict between adolescents' developmental needs for autonomy and their dependence on the family of origin for respite child care and financial, emotional, and informational support. The cost of such support tends to involve some degree of intergenerational "enmeshment" and lack of differentiation across generational boundaries. Although this degree of closeness is often requisite to the survival of the teen parent-child dyad, many teen mothers resent their parents' usurping parental authority over their grandchildren.

Group interventions were focused toward teaching the new mothers and mothers-to-be how to negotiate oral contracts between themselves and their parents, to clarify expectations, and to set the stage for negotiation of decision and task responsibilities. The costs of gaining increased authority in the role of a parent—such as giving up some precious free time to spend time with one's child, and keeping one's end of the bargain by being home on time—were discussed. Many of the teen mothers experienced ongoing conflicts with extended family support systems, and the problems associated with young parenthood and dependence were not readily solved. The group process seemed helpful, however, in moving participants toward problem formulation and the acquisition of negotiation and conflict resolution skills.

KNOWLEDGE OF CHILD DEVELOPMENT AND PARENTAL SKILLS TRAINING

Although more group time was spent on auxiliary agenda items, such as support utilization, than was originally planned, age-appropriate expectations of children were heavily emphasized. Knowledge about developmental milestones helped the mothers set realistic expectations about their children's abilities. For example, one or two of the mothers had planned to start toilet training as early as when the child reached 12 months of age. They were at least somewhat swayed when other members shared the belief that most children are not ready for this until 18-24 months of age. Teen mothers, compared with their older counterparts, tend to lack knowledge about infant development, and often have unrealistic expectations about their infants' development (Vukelich & Klerman, 1985). Accurate child development information serves to enhance the teen parent's own knowledge base and also that of others in the parent's social network who also interact with the child (Orme & Hamilton, 1987). Teen mothers are often eager to acquire information about child rearing, and they tend to share such information with aunts, uncles, and grandparents who help take care of the child.

Epstein's (1980) material on child development information needed by teen mothers of young children was utilized in the group. Mothers' knowledge about developmental milestones was checked by posing questions such as, When do most babies begin to hold out their arms to be picked up or held? Additional questions concerned when babies could be expected to do each of the following:

- feed themselves with a spoon
- cry because they are bored, and not just hungry or wet or tired
- throw toys or food on the floor because they need to show their independence
- imitate and make faces back and forth with another person
- stop eating because they want to play
- fight a diaper change because they are having too much fun moving around and exploring
- sleep through the night (that is, about eight hours)
- have a sense of humor, that is, recognize that something a little different from the usual (like a silly face) can be funny
- know whether or not their parent is in a good mood

Discussions about various sources of infant crying, temper tantrums, and noncompliant behavior among toddlers resulted in greater empathy on the part of the teen mother as to the needs of her child as opposed to her own needs. This understanding in turn led to exploration of alternatives to punishment, such as taking a time-out when the interaction between mother and child becomes conflictual. The structured and interactive methods of teaching child management skills were focused on the consequences of attending to and reinforcing desired behavior in children, giving toddlers some choices, the use of clear, concise commands, formulating workable rules, positive interaction through planned activities, and young children's needs for nurturance and stimulation.

Some of the mothers insisted on associating the age at which children understand the word *no* with expectations of complete obedience. In other words, if my child understands my words when I forbid him to touch an ashtray, he should always stop when I say no. Learned patterns of authoritarian rather than child-centered child-rearing practices were not easily interrupted. Placing the infant's need for discovery and mastery first and the mother's need to be obeyed second is a challenge for many young mothers who see themselves as primarily disciplinarians rather than as guiding the developmental skills of their offspring (Segal, 1985). Although many of the young mothers demonstrated nurturing attitudes and behavior toward their children, some leaned toward an authoritative parental style. A severely authoritarian parental style can lead to conflicts between parent and child, even to harsh discipline and child maltreatment (Robitaille, Jones, Gold, Robertson, & Milner, 1985). The goal of promoting more affectionate parental responses rather than punitive or neglectful interactions was pursued through various means, including the use of packaged parental training material.

A portion of an intervention package compiled by Mulvey and Vellenoweth (1982), particularly the section titled "Winning Ways to Talk to Children," was helpful in demonstrating ways to communicate acceptance and encouragement to children by lavish use of positive "do" statements, ways to relate to children without yelling or spanking, the impact of "poison words" on children, and the parental role in building children's self-image.

EVALUATION OF OUTCOME

An evaluation of the group intervention indicated statistically significant differences in parental attitudes toward child rearing when pre- and postintervention scores were compared ($t = -2.97$, $p < .05$). Table 8.1 depicts group members' higher mean scores after the intervention on Segal's (1985) Attitude Toward Child Rearing Measure. This 24-item scale is designed to measure child-centered and authoritarian parental attitudes. The Likert-type content of the scale includes response categories such as whether children should be allowed to ques-

Table 8.1

Group Members' Scores After Intervention

Parental Attitude	N	Mean	SD	t
Pretest	25	34.30	5.87	
Posttest	25	39.44	4.67	−2.97*

*$p < .05$.

tion the authority of their parents and the importance of providing learning experiences for children at an early age. This measure proved to be low in reliability (alpha < .60), however, so that conclusions regarding participants' change toward more child-centered parental attitudes should be made with caution.

PARENT-CHILD INTERACTION

Parental skills training, support network, and knowledge of child development help to create a child-centered as opposed to authoritarian attitude among young mothers. A positive attitude toward child rearing, one that acknowledges the child's needs for discovery and autonomy, is reflected in behavioral interactions between parent and child. Audiovisual equipment can be used to assess mother-child interactions, particularly the extent to which mothers respond to their infants' needs rather than rigidly adhere to unrealistic standards of compliance and obedience. At times, young mothers are so overwhelmed by the dual responsibilities of caring for their children and completing their education that they keep a low priority on playtime and affectionate responses toward their children. This is true particularly in cases where the mothers' parents did not model nurturing behavior to any great extent. Parental training can enhance mothers' empathy toward the nurturing needs of children. Practitioners can emphasize the need to play with, hug, and praise infants and toddlers, and they can demonstrate this type of interaction. Young mothers sometimes feel that frequent cuddling is frivolous and tends to spoil children.

Many of the teen parents in the program brought their children to the school nursery, and they were happy to participate in observational sessions that were also designed to strengthen the young mothers' interactional styles. The mothers were praised by the practitioners for talking to and hugging their children, for telling them names of objects, for permitting the children to engage in messy play, and so forth.

Scales and measures are also available for assessing the degree to which group intervention was effective in creating more child-centered parent-child interactional style. One such measure used in our teen program intervention project was Caldwell and Bradley's (1984) HOME scale. This scale assesses the quality and quantity of social, emotional, and cognitive support a mother makes available to her child. The practitioner checks off whether the parent spontaneously praises the child and conveys positive feelings toward the child, does not shout or criticize, and provides toys and learning equipment appropriate to the child's age. Originally designed for use in the home, the measure can be used in a milieu where one or two hours of observation time can be set aside to assess parent-child interactions. Toys were provided in our nursery setting, but the practitioner must keep in mind that many young mothers do not have the means to purchase many toys for their children, and this economic scarcity should not be interpreted as a negative parent-child pattern of interaction.

The Parental Acceptance-Rejection Questionnaire (PARQ) developed by Rohner (1975) has also been found to be a highly reliable instrument for measuring maternal behavior in areas of warmth and affection as opposed to neglect and indifference (Colletta, 1983). The items in the scale can also be used in parenting classes to demonstrate the range of behavior in parental acceptance. Demonstration of warmth and affection manifested by doing things to please the child include playing with, praising, singing to, caressing, hugging, or other demonstrations of love in words or actions (Rohner, 1975).

INVOLVING FATHERS

Recent studies of adolescent parenting have begun to stress the involvement of the child's father in supporting the mother-child dyad. Young fathers who cannot make substantial child support payments often can provide respite care and in-kind support (Danziger, 1988). Along the same lines, paternal grandparents can be important sources of support. Part of the intervention then is focused toward helping the adolescent maximize the involvement of the paternal family as part of the financial and task support network. Conflict resolution and planning requests for help are emphasized in similar ways as when maternal family support is utilized.

The process of support utilization is not very different when the teen mother's partner is not the father of the child. Group members discussed their expectations for reciprocity in these relationships; that is, they did expect material or other kinds of support from their partners. Peers were helpful in assessing young mothers' weighing of the costs and benefits of relationships with partners. In cases where no support was forthcoming, questions were raised regarding the advisability of continuing the relationship.

The father of the child or current partner also needs to be involved in decisions about preventing a second pregnancy. Second pregnancies may be even more unintended than are first pregnancies among teens. For those adolescents who do give birth a second time, the odds against becoming financially secure are even bleaker than for teen mothers in general.

PREVENTION OF SECOND PREGNANCIES AND LIFE OPTIONS

In cases where available support systems and community services have enabled a young mother to stay in school, a repeat birth precipitates a high probability of school dropout and a lifetime of poverty. The population of young mothers who become pregnant for a second time constitutes a large proportion of adolescent parents. Of all births to teens, 22% are repeat births (Moore, 1987).

Like teen pregnancy in general, the problem of second pregnancy prevention is much more complex than contraception and/or sex education alone can solve. A teen parent who is provided with a viable option of staying in school tends to delay second pregnancy (Children's Defense Fund, 1986). Expanding the life options available to teen mothers involves identifying such needs as academic skills training and helping with future career preparations. Some teen mothers need assistance in finding jobs while they are in school, to provide for basic needs. Working while attending school may seem too overwhelming a task for young mothers, but some do combine these roles and graduate from high school (Kissman, 1992).

In light of the fact that 80% of teenage pregnancies are unintended (Adler, Bates, & Merdinger, 1985), assessment of use of contraceptives involving the teen mother and her partner becomes an integral part of the holistic assessment of needs. A comprehensive range of support services helps adolescent parents exercise some choice about viable alternatives to repeat births.

Chapter 9

SINGLE FATHER-HEADED FAMILIES

The idea of a single father heading a family has become much more acceptable in recent years. Although the number of such families has remained at around 10% of all single-parent families (Weitzman, 1985), it is quite likely that the number and the proportion will continue to increase in the years to come. There are many reasons for this change. One of the most significant factors has to do with the changes in women's views of themselves and their roles. As options for women's lives have expanded, men's lives have been greatly affected. Women have altered the view of women's place as being beyond the traditional roles of wife and mother. Feminist thought has presented a challenge to men to explore how they lead their lives. Meth and Pasick (1990) question men's restricted notions with respect to work, family, relationships, and emotions. As women have increased their life choices to include careers outside the home, maybe even making it a choice not to parent, men have begun to think of child care, home activities, and relationships as acceptable domains for their lives. As a result, we are seeing "a trend toward greater involvement by fathers in both divorced and two-parent families" (Greif, 1985, p. 4).

In spite of the fact that there are increasing numbers of families headed by single fathers, these families face mixed reactions from other people. On the one hand, in contrast to the view of most single mothers, the man who takes on single parenting is seen as "a hero, a sympathetic figure who is admired and congratulated for his willingness and capacity to do it all" (Goodrich et al., 1988, p. 64). On the other hand, there is often a question as to how well the family is doing in terms of child care and housekeeping. These are the traditional domains of women and, in recent history, were the main reasons that fathers were not considered the parents of choice in custody cases.

As a matter of fact, clinicians find that many men report feeling uncomfortable with and ill prepared to take on these roles. It seems to be a well-accepted fact that being male does not preclude a person's being a nurturant parent, but usually neither experience nor socialization has prepared the man for such a role. This chapter explores how gender-sensitive practice based upon feminist principles can be of help with the special problems faced by single father-headed families. Many such problems stem from male socialization, and, as Ganley (1991) has suggested, feminist therapy with men is largely about resocialization.

CASE STUDY

Don W. had been a single parent of 12-year-old Steve for two years, having been granted custody in a divorce that came after 13 years of marriage. This custody arrangement had been by mutual consent of both parents, since the former Mrs. W. had a teenage daughter by a previous marriage and felt that caring for two children would be too much for her. She felt that Don would be a better parent for their son, and Steve also expressed a desire to live with his father. He saw his mother, who lived 40 miles away, every other weekend, some holidays, and several weeks in the summer.

Don had been referred by his family physician for counseling when no explanation for some physical symptoms could be found. The doctor believed stress and depression stemming from social and psychological sources were involved. Don, in the course of the initial interviews, revealed a great deal of stress around trying to balance the demands of work and of parenting. He felt he had little time for anything else. His job was demanding in terms of time and energy and was not rewarding to him emotionally, even though his salary was more than adequate.

Don was invested in being a good father to Steve and devoted most of his free time to the boy. Their time together often centered on Steve's schoolwork, and neither Don nor Steve felt there was much fun in their lives. Aside from Steve, the only meaningful relationship in Don's life was a woman friend, Cheryl, whose company he enjoyed but who was pressuring him for a commitment. She felt that Steve needed a mother and that both needed what only a woman could provide in the way of nurturing. Don quietly resented her attempts to take control over his home and the care of his son.

In the course of the first few sessions, Don talked of long-standing insecurities associated with his occupational achievements. He felt that the demands of single parenting sometimes interfered with his attaining all that he was capable of in his career. He believed that his boss and coworkers sometimes doubted his investment when he needed to attend to Steve's needs. He had never considered himself socially adept, and had always distanced himself from others. He was an only child and was essentially cut off from his parents, who lived several hundred miles away. As a result, he often felt isolated and depressed.

RESOURCES OF SINGLE FATHERS

The situation described above serves as an example of both the resources and the potential problems of single fathers with custody. In general, men go into single parenthood better equipped than women to provide for their children financially. Men are usually better able than women to maintain their predivorce standard of living. They generally have higher incomes than women and are less likely to have had their employment outside the home limited by marriage. Therefore, the shock of lowered economic status is not nearly so pronounced for the family headed by a single father as for the typical mother-headed family. This is not to overlook the fact that many single fathers feel their job performance and income sometimes suffer as they juggle parenthood and paid work.

The single father's financial resources probably allow him easier access to day care, baby-sitters, and other substitute parenting arrangements. He is probably also better able to pay for help with housework when needed, although it is not at all clear that single fathers rely on outside help to any great extent. Also, the stereotype of males as incompetent in the arena of the home can work to his advantage. Some men are able to induct female family members and women friends into "mothering" roles on the basis of such thinking. Such was the case with Don W., even though, in part, he resented the attention. In actual fact, men can come into single parenting quite capable of performing childcare and household duties, depending upon the preseparation situation.

Another resource of single fathers has to do with the fact that the majority have actively sought custody of their children. This is in contrast with women, who are simply expected to take custody and who face severe disapproval should they choose to do otherwise. Most men, not all, enter single parenthood by choice, with the strong desire to be involved with their children. In addition, these men report a high degree of confidence that they will be successful as parents (Greif, 1985).

PREPARATION FOR CHILD CARE

The resources and problems of single fathers should be examined in the context of preparation for the transition to single parenting. Feeling prepared for a major life change can often determine the seriousness of accompanying stress. When a man feels competent with child-care responsibilities and has anticipated the repercussions in other areas of his life, the stress can be minimal. Circumstances of having custody, the level of precustody involvement with his children, and resources available are all factors in his being prepared.

One of the first considerations for the practitioner in a helping role with single fathers and their families is to examine the circumstances surrounding custody. Just as with single mothers, the meanings and perceptions that are spawned by such circumstances play a significant part in the quality of relationships of the family members. How did this family come to be a family headed by a single father? How does each family member believe it affects him or her?

One of the major questions is whether the father has custody voluntarily. Mendes (1976) concludes in her study of single fathers that those who seek custody are better able to meet the demands of parenthood than those who are in the role involuntarily. Geoffrey Greif's (1985) findings generally support this view. We know that today many more men are actively seeking and receiving custody of children after separation or divorce. The court climate seems more favorable to the father's petition than in the past. Also, women now consider it more acceptable not to choose to be the custodial parent (Weitzman, Baters, Chesler, & Munger, 1986).

When the man chooses to be the custodial parent, he comes to the role with some motivation and usually has time to plan for the changes required. In those cases where the mother is in agreement about the custody choice, she has often been supportive in making such plans. Of course, this ideal circumstance of parental agreement is not always attained. There can be messy and painful custody battles that leave difficult emotional issues for the single father-headed family to face in the formative stages of its life. There are also a number of situations in which the mother has given what Greif (1985) calls "reluctant consent" (p. 39). The children may prefer to live with the father, he may offer more material security, and the mother may feel she can no longer handle the children or may simply want to avoid a court fight. Chapter 10 addresses custody and noncustodial parent issues, and these will not be dealt with extensively in this chapter. Of concern here is how the circumstance of voluntary versus involuntary custody affects the well-being of families headed by single fathers.

There are, of course, many instances in which becoming a custodial father has not been voluntary. A mother may desert the family and not maintain contact. She may decide, without consultation with her spouse, to separate and leave him with the children but to maintain contact. Certainly, this presents the remaining family with emotional and material stress for which they may have little preparation.

The level of father involvement with child care prior to separation is a significant determinant of stress, whether the single status is voluntary or nonvoluntary. Traditionally, child care and housework fall to the mother. In today's world, with women more frequently employed in work outside the home, there are more attempts at equal role sharing in the home. Nevertheless, it is still the usual case for the wife/mother to take responsibility in these areas. In some cases, as the marriage is breaking apart, the man may respond by becoming more heavily involved with the children. This is especially true if he plans to seek custody. He is more likely to gain consent from the children's mother and/or the court if he has a history of competent parenting.

Men who come by custody of their children through desertion by their mates have some characteristics in common. These fathers tend to have a higher level of involvement with child care and with housework prior to the separation (Greif, 1985). They also tend to have wives who have shared significantly in the breadwinner role, and they tend to have lower incomes than other single fathers. While they may be more experienced and engaged in child care, it does not necessarily follow that they are more effective as parents. It depends upon whether the "no choice" aspect generates feelings of resentment, bitterness, and failure. A practitioner who is sensitive to the meanings attached to being a single parent will try to surface these feelings and their implications for the whole family.

The ages and sexes of the children may also be a factor in the father's feeling of preparedness for primary custody. Men report a great deal of satisfaction in parenting younger children as opposed to adolescents (Greif, 1985). Still, men who were not heavily involved in child care prior to the divorce may need help in understanding developmental and other needs of their children. They may also require assistance in locating adequate child-care resources. Some men feel more familiar, and therefore more comfortable, with raising boys. The tasks for professionals who work with these families are to be aware of and to surface possible complications with respect to the ages and sexes of the children.

PROBLEMS OF SINGLE-FATHER CHILD CARE

Most men were not socialized to develop the nurturing, interdependent side of themselves in relationships. Most did not think of themselves as the parents primarily responsible for child care prior to their becoming primary custodial parents. Many men were brought up in traditional families in which the father provided material support and discipline but kept his emotional distance (Meth & Pasick, 1990). This model can fail them when unexpectedly life turns them into parents who must provide nurturing and emotional closeness for their children.

The single father's belief system is a significant factor in how he approaches the dual roles of nurturer and disciplinarian. In the case presented earlier, Don W. proved to be severely limited by his rigid conception of what fathers should do. His desire for a closer emotional relationship with his son was often thwarted by his thinking of himself as needing to guard his effectiveness as disciplinarian and moral teacher. His belief in hierarchy was deeply ingrained.

Certainly not all single fathers need help in learning how to nurture their children. Many men are comfortable and competent in this role, just as many women are not. When single fathers are experiencing problems in nurturing their children, socialization is often a factor. Those men who feel a great deal of anxiety about being nurturant may harbor fears of being viewed as feminine or as failures (Feldman, 1990). If they were taught that child care is "feminine," it may be extremely difficult for them to show a "softer" side through displays of affection. As Don W. explained to his son, "I often feel like hugging you. Something holds me back. My Dad always just shook hands with me. Hugging is something I'll have to learn." This was in response to his son's saying that one thing he missed about living with his mother was "the hugs."

Men are also socialized to fear failure in all endeavors, and the risk of failing in child care inhibits many men in their attempts to be more active nurturers. This fear is reinforced in many ways by society and through the popular media. It is little wonder that many single fathers are reluctant to risk exposing the untried nurturing parts of themselves if the price is possible humiliation. One possible outcome of a man's feeling that he cannot succeed in providing a satisfactory emotional climate or that it is inappropriate for a man to do so is that he will cast about for a woman to marry. He may feel he can best fulfill his responsibility to his children by providing another mother.

One client who voluntarily sought custody of his two daughters stated, "I just assumed that I would marry again quickly after my divorce so that I'd have help with the children. Kids need a mother." Many marriage counselors will bear witness to how second marriages can founder when the single father eagerly relinquishes child care to the new mother he married for the sake of his family. Practitioners must find ways to empower such men in the emotional areas of their lives if they are to be involved successfully in relationships with their children.

"The most deeply rooted intrapsychic barriers to father involvement in nurturant child care are derived from men's experience in their families of origin" (Feldman, 1990). Identification with their fathers is developmentally important for males, and they are likely to identify with the model of parenting presented by their fathers. In evaluating the nurturing aspect of child care with single fathers and their families, it is useful to examine their experiences in their families of origin. Bowen (1978) has suggested that intergenerational patterns are transmitted from one generation to another. Even though a man may vow "never to be like my father," parental styles and distancing patterns are often repeated. A practitioner can help a single father identify dysfunctional patterns and perhaps learn to make some choices as to what kind of father he wants to be. The practitioner can help a man to define these issues by asking questions such as, What did you learn from your parents about parenting that help/hinder you in your relationship with your own children?

In the case study cited earlier, Don W.'s father had been distant and emotionally unavailable during Don's childhood. Don easily fell into a parenting style in which discipline and moral development were his major concerns. The years of his marriage were spent in traditional role arrangements, so that Don was not pressured to expand his notions of parenting. Like many single fathers with custody, Don carried his "executive" role over into his new family. He organized the household well enough, but tended to rely upon Steve's mother to supply the nurturing that Steve needed. He even encouraged his son to "talk that over with your mother" when Steve approached him with a personal concern or asked advice about how to handle some difficulty with a friend. He certainly loved his son, but the feeling realm was alien and uncomfortable for him. Developing the capacity for emotional expressiveness and an acceptance of it as necessary for his own health was a central focus of change in Don's therapy.

Typically, men who become single fathers have not been extraordinary in their level of involvement with child care prior to separation and divorce. It is clear, however, that many single fathers have proven capable of expanding their fathering into nurturing when forced by circumstances to do so. It is possible that the experience of single fathers with custody can be a helpful model for all fathers.

SINGLE FATHERS AND WORK

Balancing the demands of work and family can be an extremely troublesome area for single fathers, because work is often their major identification marker. As Pasick (1990b) has noted, "So central is work to the core of most men's identities that they are usually unaware of how much time and energy they devote to planning, performing, dreaming and worrying about work" (p. 35). In many respects, men are taught to define themselves through their work. Many men believe that they express love of their families by providing for them financially and materially.

It is little wonder, then, that when a man takes on the role of primary caregiver for his children as a single father there is usually tension between the demands of paid work and home responsibilities. Women who have been in both worlds are familiar with the stress, given that, in traditional marriages, work outside the home has translated into two full-time jobs for them. For many single fathers, however, the amount of stress may come as a surprise.

Most single fathers with custody find that they must make adjustments in their work lives. For some men, more investment in parenthood comes at the cost of lesser career goals and sometimes reduced income. One father who had taken on the job of being custodial parent for three young children felt he had to lay aside his ambitions and his growing success in medical research. He found himself making impossible demands for help from his children, and he cut back his work schedule drastically. This engendered a kind of resentment that was clearly sensed by his children and led to difficulties that ultimately were addressed in family therapy.

Even when the single father gladly decides that work is secondary to his desire for parenting, there is stress. Workplaces are not particularly friendly to the needs of parents and their children. Most employers are less sympathetic to fathers than to mothers who ask to adjust schedules, take time off, or leave in emergencies to care for children. Coworkers, too, often look askance at men who seem to put the interests of their children ahead of the demands of work. For example, Don W. felt that he was definitely at a disadvantage in his work because of his child-care responsibilities. He had to refuse some assignments that involved travel. He was unable to work late and overtime when asked. He believed that this was a factor in his not receiving a promotion. He also felt that he was not well liked by coworkers who thought he was shirking his responsibilities at work. His need to be at home immediately after work also precluded his joining in social activities with fellow workers.

The practitioner can help by carefully defining issues around work and treating them seriously. Some questions to focus on include the following: What changes have you had to make in your work schedule since you took custody of the children? Had you anticipated such changes? What effect has this had on you? What were your career goals prior to custody and now? What do you miss most about your former involvement in work?

SOCIAL SUPPORT

Perhaps one of the greatest difficulties experienced by single fathers has to do with lack of adequate social support. Communities generally do not offer as much in the way of support for single fathers with custody as they do for single mothers. In addition, men tend not to have the kind of friendships with other men that are emotionally supportive (Pasick, 1990a). It would probably be rare for a single father to have male friends with whom he could share concerns about child care. Male friendships are frequently organized around activities such as golfing, playing cards, or attending sports events. For a single father the dual demands of child care and work may preclude sustaining even these relationships.

Many men depend upon women for support about "personal" problems. When men divorce, they often lose not just their wives but their best friends. Also, in most marriages, the wife has been the "social ambassador" who maintains social contacts for the couple. The single father who is not accustomed to fending for himself socially may lose much of his access to social life with separation.

Male socialization does not support the need for connectedness. Single fathers, along with other men, have been taught that being a man means being autonomous and independent. Being in the position of needing help from others may feel quite threatening to these fathers. Pasick (1990a) has suggested at least two ways in which such a belief system may prove detrimental. He notes, for one thing, that the level of social connectedness is an important determinant of health and longevity. In addition, men can develop distorted views of what is normal when they do not share deep concerns with other men. A single father who cannot share his concerns, anxieties, and fears about the responsibilities of raising children has no way to know that these feelings are not unique to him. Lack of feedback deprives him of the support that comes from knowing that others in similar circumstances share the same feelings. He is also effectively cut off from contacts that could supply useful information about how other single fathers manage their responsibilities and stress.

MASCULINITY AND SINGLE PARENTING

Practitioners who have custodial single fathers and their families as clients must be aware that most men think of therapy as antithetical to their image of masculinity (Meth & Pasick, 1990). They can be much more threatened by a referral for help than are most women. The feminist principle of therapy as an equal partnership in which the focus is on empowerment of the client is extremely helpful in allaying the anxieties of men. It is useful, too, to think in terms of providing "consultation" rather than treatment, as many family therapists have begun to do. It is also an effective "joining" measure to reframe the single father's decision to seek help as an indication of strength and determination rather than weakness (Allen & Gordon, 1990).

Certain relationship problems with his children, rigidity in ideas about the father role, and trouble in connecting appropriately to social supports may be rooted in the single father's beliefs about masculinity. When this is the case, a psychoeducational approach is recommended in the beginning. With many single fathers, it is necessary to help them "invent" a new reality about masculinity (Allen & Gordon, 1990) as a prelude to change. Problems such as those described above can be normalized and made less threatening when placed in the context of socialization.

For example, in the case situation described above, the practitioner was able to help Don W. understand how his rigid notions about masculinity restricted his ability to express many of his "softer" feelings toward his son. He could not become the nurturing father that both he and Steve desired so long as he believed that fathers were meant to be disciplinarians and problem solvers only. As with many men, Don also converted his feelings of helplessness and fear into expressions of anger. Not only did this lead to many misunderstandings between him and Steve, it also resulted in difficulties with Cheryl and with his coworkers.

The counselor helped Don to realize that society and family heritage had given him few choices about how to live his life. He was able to recognize that his beliefs need not be cast in stone. He was freed up to experiment with some new choices that would fit better and more satisfyingly into his current life. Don began to sort out and reveal his feelings and needs to significant people. For example, he was able to tell Cheryl that he did not want her to be so involved in the parenting of Steve. He defined more clearly for himself and for Steve that he wanted to have a closer, more nurturing relationship with his son.

The feminist perspective, which challenges the hierarchical model of parenting as the only correct one, can help men think in new ways about parenting. The challenge for many single fathers with custody is to blend the traditional father and mother roles so that their children are cared for materially and emotionally. They cannot leave the relationship work to women, which is an especially difficult idea for those wedded to a vision of the male role as "in charge" of discipline and rule setting.

Don W.'s philosophy was modeled after his father's oft-stated dictum, "As long as you are in my house, you live by my rules." His father tolerated no questioning of his judgments. Don had come to believe that his father was harsh sometimes, but agreed with his dad that "kids need a strong hand." He thought his father loved him, but "it was not his style to say so." He truly believed that if he let Steve know how much he cared for him he would be a less effective parent. He had decided to settle for "respect" from his son rather than love if necessary to maintain control.

Don was challenged to develop alternative beliefs about parenting. In the course of the counseling sessions, he was able to acknowledge, as many men do, a deep longing for a closer emotional relationship with his father. He did not want Steve to grow up without such a tie to him. He was helped to see that becoming more open to Steve's needs for affection and listening to Steve's side of a story would not diminish his ability to give guidance and set appropriate rules. It was slow going, but eventually Don was even able to allow his son to take some responsibility for setting rules about his own behavior. The hierarchical model shifted enough to allow for a more flexible boundary, so that Don was more available emotionally and Steve's position became more empowered.

Just as with mother-headed families, there are many examples of nonhierarchical families headed by single fathers. These are families in which children share with their fathers adult responsibilities for housework and sibling care. They often participate in decision making about rules and family activities in ways that differ from two-parent families. Whether this situation becomes problematic or not hinges on how appropriate the children's duties are and on whether the children are afforded the opportunity to be children. Older daughters in families headed by single fathers often complain of having to mother the younger children and be the father's companion. One adult daughter raised in such a family bitterly told her father, in a therapy session, how she had come to hate her two younger sisters and him for "cheating me out of my childhood." Single fathers may need help in recognizing when they are expecting too much from "parentified" daughters. Unfortunately, it is almost automatic for some men to place females in nurturing and homemaking roles.

MOURNING THE LOSSES

Robinson and Barret (1986) advise practitioners to help the single father to deal with his emotions about the loss of his marriage and all that entails. They note that practitioners should be prepared "to assist men with a wide array of feelings, ranging from loneliness and depression to self-doubt about coping as single fathers" (p. 106). Men are likely to mask grief with expressions of anger, so that losses go unmourned. They may even act out their feelings through such behaviors as sabotaging visitations between the children and their mothers.

Single fathers, such as Don W., may not even recognize the painful feelings of loss, hurt, and sadness around divorce. When Don first entered counseling, he could speak of his ex-wife only with anger and bitterness. Unfortunately, even though Don tried never to speak negatively of his ex-wife to his son, Steve was very much aware of his father's anger. He often reacted with protective statements about his mother, which, of course, added to Don's sense of rejection. Many men have trouble acknowledging the loss of their wives because this means facing "the extent of their reliance on women for emotional support" (Pasick, Gordon, & Meth, 1990, p. 165). To admit this dependence flies in the face of their beliefs about man as independent and autonomous.

It is essential for practitioners to be sensitive to the grief that underlies the anger of single fathers about the losses associated with divorce. Normalizing the difficulty of expressing their grief can be done on the grounds that most men have been taught that anger is the only intense feeling acceptable for men. To recover from the losses around divorce, single fathers must first recognize the feelings of sadness, hurt, and sometimes fear that they cannot make it on their own. The therapist can sometimes help by revisiting the story of the separation and divorce with the focus on feelings rather than on facts. Reframing of anger as sadness and hurt can help elicit those feelings. Discussing how divorce brings with it loss of companionship and social contact, which leads to current feelings of loneliness, can help. The helping professional should keep in mind that the divorced father may be grieving not just the loss of a marriage but the loss of a dream and an image about the ideal family that he can no longer have. It is also productive to explore how the current loss is reminiscent of his reactions to past losses in his life. Divorce can trigger much unresolved grief from the past for these men.

Single fathers with custody of their children may also need to mourn changes in their work lives. Altering career goals and/or making work outside the home a secondary priority to parenting can be a change of major proportions for men. Practitioners can be of real help simply by surfacing and accepting these feelings, which sometimes can be very ambivalent. Other losses, such as loss of freedom in social contacts, also need to be aired. It may be helpful for the practitioner to ask questions such as, What did you have to give up to take on custody of your children? and How do you think your life would be different if you did not have primary care of your children?

BUILDING A SOCIAL SUPPORT SYSTEM

Much of what the discussion offered in Chapter 6 applies also to helping men build needed social supports. Practitioners who have single fathers for clients do well to focus on the support systems available, using the ecomap and other network assessment techniques discussed in earlier chapters of this book. It is especially important in work with single fathers to surface those beliefs about masculinity that may prove to be obstacles in building the support system necessary for the well-being of these fathers and their families.

Greif (1985) stresses that the need for single fathers to have the opportunity to meet with other single parents is of utmost importance. Practitioners may find that their clients need help in getting connected to organizations such as Parents Without Partners. Churches may have groups especially for single parents. The development in recent years of fathers' groups (Gordon, 1990a), men's support groups, and men's therapy groups that focus on their emotional lives will be valuable to many single fathers.

EXTENDED FAMILY AS SUPPORT

Chapter 5 deals with the single parent and familial support. With single fathers, however, it is particularly important to help them understand the immense influence their fathers have on the way they parent their own children. "The exploration of one's relationship to his father can be used to help a man determine the kind of husband, father, friend, etc. he wants to be" (Gordon, 1990b, p. 246).

The practitioner in the Don W. case helped Don to revisit his relationship with his father. Much of this was done in the presence of Steve, because hearing the story of this aspect of his father's life helped him to gain a more empathic view of his father's struggles. As Don realized how he had missed his father's attention in his childhood, he was able to open up to Steve much more. He was able to spend more "playful" time with his son, and they began to enjoy each other's company.

Don did not have an easy time discussing his father, because there was much pain in the relationship. A genogram along with questions structured the discussions. In the process of Don's gathering information from his father, some important reconnecting was begun. Don's father had been divorced prior to his marriage to Don's mother. Don was able to talk to his father about his feelings about divorce, which opened up communication in ways never possible before. His father surprisingly began to be an emotional support in the lives of both Don and Steve.

THERAPIST'S STANCE

Helping professionals must bring an open mind to work with single fathers. Men can parent children well and comfortably, and increasing numbers are choosing to do so. As they do, more real options concerning custody will be opened for women. This chapter has discussed some special aspects of single father-headed families that can present problems. A major area of change often has to do with male socialization. Feminist principles employed by therapists can be helpful with single fathers as well as with single mothers. One goal of therapy with single fathers, as with all men, "is to help a man to construct a reality in which he can comfortably incorporate these more 'feminine' parts of himself into his life story" (Allen & Laird, 1991, p. 96).

Chapter 10

NONCUSTODIAL PARENTING

Many noncustodial parents who wish to be more involved in parenting their children face multiple barriers, ranging from lack of skills in parenting at a distance to legal custody disputes. The dynamics surrounding autonomy and connectedness in any family, where members are striving to maintain a comfortable balance between closeness and distance from each other, are not resolved when parents divorce. Interventions to alleviate parental conflicts often must center on authority over visiting rights, financial support, and other child-rearing issues to assure continuity of care arrangements for the children.

The best child-care arrangement usually involves an active role on the part of the absentee parent. Interventions are aimed at overcoming obstacles in the noncustodial parent-child relationship in cases where the child has sided with the custodial parent during the separation and divorce process. Bringing in the peripheral parent, usually the father, to strengthen the support network of the family system is an important component of network intervention.

Gender differences in noncustodial parenting include a more negative view of the mother who voluntarily or involuntarily relinquishes custody. Self-help groups can be extremely helpful in validating the experiences of noncustodial mothers and in raising consciousness about societal sanctions of nonconformity to rigid gender roles. Individual and group interventions are often aimed at dealing with guilt, blame, reestablishing relationships with the children, referrals to legal and economic resources, and creating new support networks.

For fathers, who constitute the majority of noncustodial parents, the experience of guilt and blame associated with unfit parenthood is not as severe as for mothers. Interventions, however, are also aimed at dealing with family loss and feelings of victimization. Fathers often lack skills in maintaining or reestablishing relationships with their children, because many have not been expected to play an active role in coparenting or parenting at a distance.

PARENTING AT A DISTANCE

Research suggests that cooperative relationships between estranged parents enhance the adjustment of the children after divorce (Lowery & Settle, 1985). Parenting at a distance is a viable option for some parents, but this requires open communication with both the children and the estranged spouse. When at all possible, the practitioner needs to help parents work together to facilitate contacts between the children and the noncustodial parent. Mutually beneficial contacts can be developed, ranging from correspondence to weekend visits and even more joint-type custody.

In the best situations, shared parental responsibilities contribute to the success of the binuclear family, where children are parented by separated spouses rather than by a single parent. Even in cases where geographical distance limits the flexibility of absentee parent contacts, "summer custody" provides respite for the custodial parent and a closer relationship between absentee parent and child. The family actually continues after divorce, held together through joint parental responsibilities.

Interventions aimed at increased effectiveness in parenting at a distance must be highly dependent on the goals of treatment, however. A declining relationship between a noncustodial parent and the children, for example, may indicate the need for family therapy. The permission of the custodial parent for visitation rights must be secured, and the children, if they are old enough, ideally are included in this decision. The goals of this type of intervention could involve helping parents to feel more competent when they are with the children, clarifying communication among family members, and helping individuals adjust to new visitation arrangements.

Parental relationships can be so conflictual, however, that any attempts to intervene in the family system can prove defeating. Therapy that aims to strengthen the capacity of the noncustodial parent to be involved with the children should be approached with careful attention to the wishes of everyone involved and the mediation of conflicting needs of all members of the binuclear family.

Both peer support groups and individual interventions can provide needed informational support regarding role clarification and how to enhance relationships with the children and estranged spouse. Information about needed resources includes referrals to public and private agencies and groups that are available to help parents with specific problems of child custody, child snatching, emotional support, legal aid, and child support payments. In some cases custody issues are not permanently resolved, and these issues coincide with the need of many noncustodial parents to rebuild support networks and social contacts.

Emotional ventilation and role clarification for those parents who are having difficulty adjusting to the absentee parent role can begin in a group setting of supportive peers. Many members of the Parents Without Partners organization are noncustodial parents. Group chapters exist in virtually every large metropolitan area and offer various social and educational programs that can help rebuild social networks. Other parenting groups designed as means of support and self-help have been established in local communities. Parenting Network and Parenting Together are two such groups that offer parental skills training and mutual support.

Network assessment and intervention involves informal support systems as well. For single parents in general, a major adjustment following divorce often includes replacing existing networks that are no longer supportive and creating new ones.

MEETING THE CHILDREN'S NEEDS

Intervention with the binuclear family is centered on the children's needs more than on the unresolved conflicts between parents. Mediation ranges from negotiating time sharing of caregiving responsibilities to contract agreements regarding financial support. A workable child-rearing plan is the ideal way to ensure some degree of continuity of care for children in cases where both parents have actively participated in taking care of the child. Fathers who share custody of their children in summers, for example, help maintain a strong child-father relationship and a more regular family pattern of coparenting.

As is the case with two-parent families, peripheral fathers should be strongly encouraged to assume greater responsibility for the care of their children. Lack of interest in the children seems directly related to fathers' failure to contribute to their financial support, and it is most frequently the husband who refuses contact in parental visitation arrangements (Arendell, 1986). Practitioners need to maintain strong expectations for paternal involvement in child rearing. Mothers should be encouraged to assert their right to respite care by placing the children in their father's care whenever possible. Redefining an ongoing relationship with the absentee parent can be a painful experience for both parents. Coparenting, however, can benefit children in indirect as well as direct ways. Mothers who are able to get some respite from the heavy demands of dual caretaker/wage earner roles, for instance, have more energy left to devote to parenting.

At a conference held in New York City in 1986 called "Mothers on Trial: The Politics of Child Custody," the mothers offered the following advice to noncustodial mothers (Takas, 1987). These suggestions apply to absentee fathers as well:

1. Talk to your children. Let them know that you will always love them, no matter what happens.
2. Let them be sad. Let them be angry, even angry with you. If they can show their hurt and anger, it's because they trust you.
3. If you lose custody, it will be painful to see your children. See them anyway. After a while, new routines will develop. The hurt decreases.

In her novel *The Good Mother,* Miller (1986) describes a mother who loses custody and who puts on a happy face while her child clings to her and begs to stay. In order to shield her child from the pain of separation, the mother never explains that she, too, wishes the child could stay.

Until recently, studies of the effects of divorce on children have been confined to the father-absent family, and especially the effects on boys who are living in the custody of their mothers (Clingempeel & Repucci, 1982). More recent evidence suggests that sole custody may be more functional for same-sex children; boys scored higher on social functioning when they stayed with their fathers (Lowery & Settle, 1985). The implications of such findings for noncustodial parenting are that, whenever possible, absentee fathers should be encouraged to be especially involved with their male children. Boys are socialized to maintain a great distance from their mothers during adolescence. Although the functional aspects of gender developmental differences are open for debate, the responsibility of absentee fathers to share in caregiving activities during their children's adolescence should be especially encouraged.

GENDER AND CUSTODY DECISIONS

The prevailing legal standard for awarding custody during most of this century was the "doctrine of tender years," which presumed that a child would be better off with the mother, unless she was unfit (Doudna, 1982). An unfit mother could be anything from a child abuser to an alcoholic or adulteress. When the movement for sexual equality under the law extended to custody issues, judges increasingly began to find that maternal preference discriminated against men. Most courts have now replaced the tender years doctrine with a theoretically nonsexist guideline. The parent who is awarded custody in disputed cases is simply the one who serves the best interests of the child (Doudna, 1982). And in many cases, that has turned out to be the financially more capable parent, the father.

In the most extreme cases, a mother loses custody of her children through more violent means, that is, through the abduction of the children by the spouse. This problem is becoming alarmingly more common as custody disputes become increasingly bitter (Chesler, 1986). Unfortunately, the "unfit" stereotype still haunts many noncustodial mothers, no matter the circumstances surrounding the custody arrangements.

Gender differences in parental roles dictate that custodial fathers be seen as heroes while noncustodial mothers tend to receive very negative feedback for having "abandoned" their children. A large number of absentee mothers perceive no element of choice in the custody decision because of economic factors (Paskowics, 1982). Mothers who head one-parent families earn less than 50% as much as fathers who head male-headed custodial households, even when these women work full-time (U.S. Bureau of the Census, 1985). Although women, as a group, earn 64% of male wages (Cetron, Rocha, & Rebecca, 1988), the drastic 73% average reduction in the standard of living following divorce (Weitzman, 1985) suggests that the decision to relinquish custody is often closely tied to economic conditions. Mothers who do retain custody are thus frequently impoverished, and more than half of all children living in poverty are in households headed by women (Walters, 1988).

ABSENTEE FATHERS

Absentee fathers constitute the vast majority of absentee parents. Although fathers are increasingly awarded custody of their children, 87% of divorced or separated mothers were awarded custody in 1985 (U.S. Bureau of the Census, 1985). Several studies have reported that noncustodial fathers experience significant emotional distress as a result of reduced contact with their children or their marginal parenthood (Keshet & Rosenthal, 1988). Although paternal relinquishment of custody is much more normative than is maternal relinquishment, treatment issues with absentee fathers do involve dealing with loss, victimization, lack of skills in parenting at a distance, and establishing new support networks.

The paternal role has traditionally been characterized as primarily disciplinarian in nature (Feldman, 1990). With changing gender roles, men increasingly are learning to nurture and to become more involved with their children. Lacking role models and the requisite attitudes and skills to parent effectively, some males come into treatment to learn to become more sensitive to their children's needs.

Practitioners can role model how to engage in affectionate responding, praising, and play with young children. Suggestions for activities, outings, and even meal preparation are sometimes needed. Fathers who have been underinvolved with their children need to learn to diffuse rigid boundaries that have kept them insensitive to their children's needs. Fathers tend to be socialized into the role of the disengaged parent by their own fathers, who distanced themselves from their children. This arrangement may be facilitated by mothers who do not wish to relinquish the nurturing role to fathers. At the risk of appearing to engage in mother blaming, it should be noted that some custodial mothers may even sabotage efforts of visiting fathers in order to retain their primary role as the involved parent (Gordon, 1990a).

Realistically, interventions aimed at facilitating more active and nurturing father involvement are likely to be rather piecemeal until a more accepting attitude evolves toward shared parenthood and fathers' responsibilities toward the emotional as well as financial needs of their children. Societal values that dictate parental roles and responsibilities are changing very slowly. Osherman (1986) notes that despite the rapid increase in the number of fathers who are present in the delivery room when their infants are born, only 50% of fathers visit their children regularly following divorce, and only 20% of the children of divorce see their fathers once a week or more.

Well-meaning friends and relatives often assume that fathers who do spend time alone with their children are "just baby-sitting" rather than parenting. Fathers are increasingly seeking active participation in custody decisions. A group of fathers who have formed a national organization to assert their rights in custody disputes are effecting some changes to increase fathers' involvement in joint, split, and sole custody decisions.

Gordon (1990a) concludes that practitioners often need to explore the issue of lack of father involvement rather than assume that fathers do not wish to maintain contact with their children. Painful feelings associated with separation must be confronted. Many fathers have difficulty conceptualizing their relationships with their children as distinct from the relationships they had with their spouses. Parental separation is then associated with estrangement from the children as well.

There are tremendous social reinforcements associated with paternal involvement, and this can be emphasized to encourage fathers to be more active in parenting their children. Children whose fathers are disengaged and fail to take interest in their lives often feel rejected, which results in low self-esteem and even acting-out behavior. Feldman (1990) offers the following case example relating to this type of problem and intervention with a mother-son dyad where the father was peripheral.

The divorced mother of a 13-year-old boy ("Andy") requested therapy because of her son's oppositional behavior at school (his grades were extremely poor because he would not do homework or study for tests) and at home (he refused to participate in household chores and was extremely irritable and argumentative). The father was peripheral; he visited once or twice a month (irregularly) and phoned occasionally.

During the initial evaluation interviews, it quickly became apparent that Andy harbored a great deal of resentment toward his father for being "the cause of the divorce" and for "abandoning" him after the divorce. His passive-aggressive behavior was, to a large degree, a way of getting his father's attention and expressing his resentment toward him. Andy was struggling with painful feelings of worthlessness and helplessness, derived to a large degree from his perception that his father did not love or value him.

Andy's father expressed concern about his son's behavioral problems and criticized his wife for not disciplining him more effectively. He perceived himself as too busy with his work to be able to spend as much time with his son as he would like to. In therapy, Andy was able to talk with his father about some of his feelings of resentment and anger. The father was initially defensive, but over time was able to empathize with his son's underlying pain and longing for a relationship with him. He began to increase the frequency of his phone calls and visits. Initially, Andy was resistant to these initiatives, experiencing them as "too little, too late." Eventually, however, he softened, and the father-son relationship began to improve. As this happened, Andy's oppositional behavior diminished, and his mood improved.

It is important to note that mediation between father and son and encouragement of the father's involvement is not analogous to bringing the father in as rescuer or pathologizing the situation in which a son had minimal "male role modeling." Rather, the father was expected to take an active role in coparenting in a binuclear family, which is increasingly seen as one of many norms among diverse family forms. Obstacles to the father's involvement, such as overtime at work, are not seen as insurmountable.

Children's resentment and hesitancy to become involved with the absentee parent may subside quickly as the father-child relationship is reestablished. In many cases, however, intervention with the family involves a much more in-depth focus on the dynamics of the triad relationship, including the tendency of the child to side with the custodial parent.

ABSENTEE MOTHERS

Gender differences related to parental roles are relevant to interventions with absentee parents. The pejorative social status of the mother-headed family does not begin to describe the negative status of the absentee mother, whose nontraditional gender role conjures up mother blaming at its worst. While women in general have been expanding their gender roles into nontraditional occupations, the position of the noncustodial mother remains far removed from social norms and expectations. Noncustodial mothers are still generally highly disapproved of, even if they gave up custody unwillingly. Many people assume such women are unfit mothers, and many face societal hostility (Doudna, 1982).

The number of women who have given up custody of their minor children is increasing; it is currently estimated to be between 500,000 and one million (Weitzman et al., 1986). These estimates may be low, because remarriage by either parent results in a family's being absorbed into other categories, such as reconstituted families.

Therapists must be aware of their own biases concerning motherhood. Negative stereotypes that reflect societal attitudes toward noncustodial mothers are not likely to be helpful to the therapeutic process. Rather, a holistic, multidimensional perspective that recognizes the problematic interface between the noncustodial mother and the environment in which she interacts is imperative. The problems associated with the status of noncustodial mothers are closely linked to the social status of women in general. Rapid changes in women's roles often create negative evaluation of nonconventional role performance, even on the part of helping professionals.

Greif and Pabst (1988), in a survey of 517 noncustodial mothers, identified low self-esteem, lack of clear role definition, victimization, and rejection from the children as some of the areas of clinical focus. Because the mothering role has been much more entrenched in the self-identity of women who parent, problems in categorizing the ambivalent status of the noncustodial mother, who is neither childless nor a mother in the conventional sense, have relegated her to a deviant status. She may need help in redefining her own identity as a part of an unconventional system of binuclear, joint, or split mother and father custodial families, or even apart from the institution of motherhood. Whether she finds her "centrality" in the midst of a supportive milieu of similar peers or as a parent who takes an active part in the lives of her children, she must work toward normalizing her deviant status before she can make long-range educational or career plans.

The needs of the noncustodial mother sometimes are not unlike those of displaced homemakers who are unprepared to face the abrupt shift from family life to the more public world of the "swinging single," individuals who often rely heavily on extrafamilial support systems. The "swinging single" label is particularly problematic for mothers who fail to pledge their allegiance to the dogma of selflessness associated with child rearing because they are often stereotyped as cold-hearted, self-centered, or sexually promiscuous (Paskowics, 1982). Mothers who relinquish custody still bring out what Walters (1988) refers to as societal dichotomization of a mother as nurturer/caretaker versus sexual and self-directed individual. The goal of interventions with noncustodial parents, and mothers in particular, therefore centers on enabling them to make a forward move from victimization and feelings of rejection toward role clarification and continued personal growth.

It is important to note that noncustodial mothers are not a homogeneous group, and a full one-third report few or no problems in adjustment to the role of absentee mother (Greif, 1987). Distinctions need to be made, also, between mothers who need help in working through feelings of victimization after having given up the battle for custody and those who are ready to move ahead toward self-development and growth. In most cases, however, these women can be empowered by a support system that reframes their experiences as normative and confronts guilt and self-blame as part of a broader context in which women live.

Individualization of the status of noncustodial mothers also involves normalizing the experiences of those mothers who have voluntarily given up custody of their children. This could present the greatest challenge to therapists who have no problem understanding the circumstances of mothers who were forced to relinquish custody, but who lack empathy for those who voluntarily relinquished or were judged unfit. Although the circumstances leading to a "voluntary" relinquishment often present little choice, therapists must evaluate their own ability to affirm a mother's choice to have the children's father take primary responsibility for child rearing.

SELF-HELP GROUPS

Peer support groups may need professional leadership in dealing with scapegoating and mother blaming of those mothers who have chosen noncustodial status. Anecdotal evidence from group practice indicates that members who have voluntarily relinquished custody are sometimes blamed by those who feel victimized as a result of being forced to give up custody. Self-help groups, however, have the potential to provide critical means to empower the role of the absentee mother by universalizing her experience. Mutual-aid groups can enhance mothers' self-esteem by creating a common bond that helps to clarify the difficult role of mothering at a distance. Among the available resources for supportive networks is a group called Mothers Without Custody, a mutual self-help program established in the 1970s to seek out and support noncustodial mothers.

Both group and individual interventions tend to focus on reframing relinquishment or loss of custody in a positive way, and on dealing with a sense of powerlessness and loss. Mothers who have been able to negotiate mutually rewarding parenting-at-a-distance contracts and to process through the initial period of grief and loss are better prepared to focus on their own career development and rebuilding of their social networks. For noncustodial mothers, partnered friends and relatives who are still supportive following relinquishment are often few in number. Social isolation can present a threat to these mothers' psychological well-being at a time when emotional support is sorely needed to facilitate the transition to a difficult role. Noncustodial mothers may need help in creating new support that can buffer the stress associated with rejection and the self-recrimination that sometimes prompts them to hide the fact that they are parents. Noncustodial mothers have reported being met with icy glares and even insults when they revealed their parental status.

Chapter 11

POLICY PERSPECTIVES

Gender-sensitive practice is based on a contextual view of environmental influences on the quality of women's lives. If individual-environmental interactions are partly gender based, to what extent do social policies respond to changing roles of women as sole wage earners and caregivers? Because a large proportion of the poverty population are impoverished mothers and their children, antipoverty policies responsive to this population of single parents must be both holistic and multidimensional. These policies need to be based on a gender-specific perspective of mothers' employment as it interrelates with child care, health care, and other comprehensive child welfare services.

Social policies in the past have been based on the assumption that a minimum-wage job meets basic needs for mother-headed families. However, mothers who provide sole support for their families need to earn at least $6-$7 per hour order to meet the basic needs of their families and also pay for child care, transportation, and other work-related expenses (Bane et al., 1989).

Comparisons across cultures are particularly relevant when we look at those systems that are making considerable progress in reducing poverty among the most vulnerable group, that of single parents and their families. Homogeneity and small population size in the Scandinavian countries, for example, serve to facilitate class and gender equality in the distribution of resources. Long-standing values of social responsibility for the welfare of individuals at the bottom rung of the economic hierarchy are now extended specifically to women and children because, although women are increasingly choosing not to parent, a substantial proportion of those who do are sole providers for their children and many are poor.

In this chapter we discuss the link between the persistent gender gap in earnings across cultures and child and family welfare. In response to the relatively low earning capacity of women, Scandinavian social policies are seeking to integrate traditionally distinct policy areas such as wage labor and child welfare. In Norway, as in other Scandinavian countries, the interface between wage labor and child welfare is being defined as gender specific because it is women who are mainly in charge of reproduction. It is women who most often combine reproductive and productive labor—that is, childbirth/child rearing and paid wage labor. Integrative wage labor and child welfare policies are therefore in the best interests of women.

It is no coincidence that policy areas viewed as overlapping rather than distinct are in keeping with the multidimensional and holistic thinking advocated by feminist principles. The point has been raised by feminist scholars, however, that social policies that respond to the needs of women and children create dependency on the "patriarchal" welfare state, which only reinforces the dependency relationship women have had with men (Hernes, 1984). Until greater wage parity exists between males and females, however, and until gender differences in parental responsibilities are shared more equally, the state must fill the gap and ensure a decent quality of life for women and children.

The ideology upon which family policies are based in Scandinavia is that harder choices should not be forced on women than on men or greater sacrifices when they combine child care and paid work activities (Bohorst & Sirin, 1986). The "woman-friendly state" is a benevolent and socially responsible state responsive to the reality that women and children make up the largest proportion of impoverished individuals worldwide. Such a state strives toward equality by formulating redistributive policies and support services in response to the reality that women spend disproportionate amounts of time performing unpaid work by way of child care, and they often do not earn sufficient wages to raise their families above the poverty level.

Finally, we discuss how the Family Support Act of 1988 has been implemented to respond to multiple needs of impoverished women and children in the United States. This policy, described as "the first significant change in the welfare system in 53 years," provides education and

work training, child-care and health coverage, child support enforcement, and other comprehensive family services for recipients of AFDC
benefits (*Hunger Action Forum*, 1990). We point out some of the limitations of the Family Support Act, which responds to the needs of
approximately one-fourth of AFDC recipients eligible for services and
does not address the needs of working poor families. For working poor
families, recent expansion of earned income tax credits and medicaid
for poor children are intended to help the 21% of families headed by
employed women who have incomes below the poverty level (Pearce,
1990).

GENDER GAP IN
EARNINGS AND CHILD WELFARE

Future predictions about a narrowing gender gap in earnings will
have important consequences for the large proportion of mother-headed
families who are impoverished. Women, who now earn on the average
less than 70% of male wages, are predicted to increase their average
earnings to 85% of male wages by the year 2000 (Cetron et al., 1988).
Because single mothers tend to be employed in the lower-paying service
sector in even greater proportions than are women in general (Fox &
Hesse-Biber, 1984), optimistic predictions about increased resources
and improved quality of life for mother-headed families must be made
with caution. This is true especially in light of recent statistics indicating that households maintained by men or married couples experienced
a decrease in poverty while single-parent families experienced an increased rate of poverty in the 1980s (U.S. Bureau of the Census, 1989b).

Cross-nationally, persistent gender stratification of the labor force,
such that women are segregated in the lower strata of all occupational
categories, cannot be accounted for wholly by gender differences in
education, work tenure and experience, or muscle power. Women may
"prefer" lower-paying occupations because they are expected to perform
lower-paying work. Although women's education tends to be interrupted in cases of early childbearing, lower education level does not
account for the wide gender-based discrepancy in wages. That single
mothers are employed in marginal work due to their multiple roles as
sole providers and caregivers and are therefore less desirable as employees
is what Bane et al. (1989) refer to as a discrimination hypothesis.

Under the guise of protection against work that is overdemanding on the time and energy of the single parent, women who parent, and particularly women who parent alone, are often marginalized in the labor market. Paradoxically, low-paying work tends to afford less flexibility for caregivers to take time off when children are ill than do many higher-paying professional occupations.

For single mothers of color, wage equality seems even further away than for their white counterparts, whose earnings are not as low when compared with those of white males. Nearly one-third of black single mothers who worked for pay in 1987 were below the poverty level, while 17% of white single mothers in the labor market were poor (U.S. Bureau of the Census, 1989a). Gender and ethnic wage inequalities create a need for compensatory policies and more equitable distribution of resources to ensure a decent standard of living for women and children (Figueira-McDonough & Sarri, 1987).

In addition to wage parity, comprehensive child-care policies, including mothers allowance, child support payments, health care, and quality day care, are needed to raise mother-headed families out of poverty. These comprehensive child-care policies are referred to in Scandinavia as reproductive policies. Reproductive policies respond to the needs of diverse family systems, where mothers are most often employed, and particularly to impoverished single-parent families.

INTEGRATIVE POLICY PERSPECTIVES

Integrative policies that redress low wages and lack of resources for impoverished mothers and children are developing at a much faster rate in Scandinavia than in the United States. Scandinavian social policies are integrative in that they focus on the interface between the care functions and labor force participation of women. Legislative proposals to shorten work hours for women caregivers to 30 hours per week, for example, are viewed as part of a comprehensive child welfare package. In Norway, proposals have been made for public transfers through social security benefits to cover income forgone through shorter work hours.

Without the cooperation of the corporate sector, however, wage labor policies that advocate for the welfare of women caregivers and wage earners have limited impact (Hernes, 1987). Benevolent and woman-friendly state policies are certainly mediated by wage earners' dependency on the market demand for labor, so that countries with lower unemployment have much greater success in integrating wage labor and child welfare policies.

For sole providers, most often mothers, who are not in the labor market, income transfers such as mothers allowance and cash benefits are part of the social security system rather than public welfare in Scandinavia. Mothers allowance benefits are paid to all mothers with dependent children, and money received through the social security system may carry less stigma than does public assistance in this country. However, similar problems exist for Norwegian mothers who are making the transition from income transfer recipient status to wage labor as for their U.S. counterparts who are getting off of AFDC benefits. Namely, when benefits are cut off too soon, working mothers are caught in a "poverty trap": They are not earning sufficient wages to raise their families' standard of living (Hatland, 1984). Current changes in income transfer benefits in Norway include higher income disregards, so that single parents who enter the labor market do not lose all benefits before they can establish themselves in the labor market.

Problems associated with loss of benefits in the transitional phase when mothers are entering wage labor are compounded in the United States, where lack of national health care coverage creates a greater loss of benefits for families trying to make a transition from AFDC recipient status to wage labor.

COMPREHENSIVE CHILD WELFARE POLICIES

Comprehensive child welfare policies in Norway reflect an integrative view of maternal and child welfare and of reproductive and "productive" work. Reproductive work and women's issues center on that life phase when a great deal of energy is devoted to child-rearing activities. The juncture between reproductive and productive labor is a critical area of market, state, and family policies. The interconnections among these traditionally distinct policy dimensions have strong bearing on reproductive policies that respond to what are referred to in Scandinavia as "organization of life" issues (Kissman, 1991). For a vast majority of individuals, these issues center on child-rearing and wage-earning activities. Until gender roles evolve more fully to include males in caregiving activities, this is especially true for women.

Reproductive policies responding to organization of life issues include parental leave. Parental leave policies apply to a greater extent to two-parent families than to single parents, who tend to be more concerned with child support enforcement and adequate wages that enable a sole supporter to provide for her family. Norway does have, however, up to 168 days per child parental leave, which can be divided between parents (*Minifacts on Equal Rights,* 1989).

Quality child care is imperative for all working mothers with young children. Single parents in Norway have a priority on day-care spaces for their children because basic survival needs are at stake for working mothers whose families depend on their income alone (Leira, 1987). Quality child care is an important part of a comprehensive child welfare package in Norway, where municipal child care is available for only 60% of children needing care (Leira, 1987). Child care in Norway lags behind that in other Scandinavian countries. The United States is even further behind, and is among only five developed nations in the world that lack national child-care policies (Lubeck & Garrett, 1988).

These and other concerns affecting the welfare of women who parent alone require that a distinction be made between organization of life or reproductive issues, often referred to as "women's issues," and equality policies. Equality policies, which mandate equal pay for equal work, do not address the need for services, such as comprehensive child care, that can create adequate infrastructure for mothers to move from the status of public assistance recipients to work force participants.

When gender is identified as a social category, some equality policies become gender specific, and the boundaries separating family, child welfare, and wage labor policies become diffused. The integration of these traditionally distinct policy areas is desirable because rigid boundaries serve as barriers to gender equality in the labor market and quality care for children.

MOTHERS ALLOWANCE
AND CHILD SUPPORT ENFORCEMENT

The rate of poverty among women and children is higher in the United States than in Scandinavia. Although the Scandinavian countries have not eradicated poverty, the poverty rate among Norwegian children, for example, is 9%, compared with 20% in the United States (Danziger, 1989; Kamerman & Kahn, 1988). Some 50% of children who live in mother-headed families in the United States live in poverty (Danziger, 1989). The high rate of poverty among American children cannot be accounted for by family size, higher proportion of single parents, or any demographic characteristic other than lower income transfers compared with other countries where the proportion of single-parent families is high (Kamerman & Kahn, 1989).

Income transfers by way of mothers allowance and child support payments are two components of comprehensive child welfare policies more common in other countries than in the United States. A modest mothers allowance benefit paid to all mothers in 117 Western industrial countries, but not in the United States (Hewlett, 1986), helps to reduce child poverty. Child support payments also serve to reduce child poverty in Scandinavia, where more than 90% of single-parent families receive child support payments (Hatland, 1984). In Norway, the state pays child support to mothers and then collects the money from fathers. As of 1989, according to census figures, 40% of single-parent families in the United States did not even have a child support award. Of those that did, just over half actually received the full amount on a regular basis; a quarter received partial payment, and the rest got nothing (U.S. Bureau of the Census, 1989a).

ANTIPOVERTY POLICIES:
THE FAMILY SUPPORT ACT OF 1988

In the United States, the Family Support Act of 1988 is intended to address child support enforcement, child care, and wage labor among recipients of Aid to Families with Dependent Children. Stricter child support enforcement is often not feasible in the United States, however, because of high unemployment and underemployment, especially among young African-American and Latino males. One judge noted, for example, that even if he mandated 70% of a man's wages for child support, it would not be sufficient to raise his children's standard of living above the poverty level (*Hunger Action Forum,* 1990). Requiring courts to review support awards every three years and garnisheeing the paychecks of absentee parents who are ordered to pay support will help some families, but many will still be left without support payments.

Ethnic and class inequality are a part of the larger context that serves to limit financial resources for women and children. This is one of the reasons that advocacy for the welfare of all citizens is an important part of a broad feminist agenda across cultures (Kissman, 1991).

WAGE LABOR

The Family Support Act of 1988 sets out programs for work training, child care, and health services for AFDC recipients. The Job Opportunities and Basic Skills (JOBS) program requires states to provide education, job training, and job search help to young parents and long-term AFDC recipients. States must also provide child-care and transportation funds to participants. Working mothers who have been receiving AFDC benefits are able to retain health services for one year, for example, during the transition period when they are establishing themselves in the labor force. In the absence of employee health care benefits, however, these families are not likely to raise their wages sufficiently to cover major or even minor health care services.

Another limitation of the program lies in the high unemployment in some areas of the country. In other areas, such as Napa County, California, participants are receiving more than $7 per hour on the average (*Hunger Action Forum,* 1990). Part of the program's success has been that educational services must include courses leading to a high school equivalency degree, basic literacy training, and English-as-a-second-language classes for those who need them. Several states will also pay for AFDC recipients to attend two- or four-year colleges.

Some opposition has been raised concerning the practice of forcing mothers of young children to enter the labor market. No society places a high value on caregiving activities as socially necessary labor (Dahl, 1985). As increasing numbers of mothers of young children voluntarily enter the labor market, objections to mandates for public assistant recipients to enter wage labor may become less relevant. And AFDC recipients who oppose entering wage labor and who choose to stay home to raise their children often do so in response to lack of affordable child care and lack of adequate wages to pay for health care and transportation.

LEGISLATION AND FAMILY POLICIES

The Family Support Act of 1988 was designed to help AFDC recipients get off public assistance; it is limited in helping poor working families whose standard of living does not meet basic needs, including adequate health care, quality day care, and even a diet that meets minimum nutritional standards. For these families, policies that have stronger mandates for gender parity in wages, education and training, child care, health care benefits, and transportation allowances are sorely needed.

Recent expansion of medicaid for children is a step in the right direction, but still leaves the family economically vulnerable because it does not extend coverage to the family's sole wage earner. Other recent expansions in benefits for impoverished families include childcare and income tax credits for low-income families. The long-awaited child-care bill passed by Congress mandates $2.5 billion in grants to the states to allow them to subsidize child-care programs especially for families who are receiving AFDC benefits or are in danger of going on welfare because they cannot afford child care (*Hunger Action Forum,* 1991). The earned income tax credit for working families with children is an income refund paid to families whose incomes are below $20,000 per year. Mother-headed families represent a high proportion of these families. The maximum payment, now $953, will rise to $1,700 for a family with two children by 1994 (*Hunger Action Forum,* 1991).

These current policy changes representing successful approximation toward comprehensive family policies are based more on the need to reduce welfare rolls than on any understanding of the gender-specific nature of poverty as it relates to single-parent families, including working poor families. Policies based on egalitarian values upholding the rights of all individuals for basic needs would require consciousness-raising about the reality that a large proportion of families are going to remain mother-headed. Among the obstacles to be overcome in the process of moving toward societal acceptance of diverse family forms is wishful thinking that somehow single parenting can be drastically reduced. Suggestions for policies aimed at accomplishing this even include discouraging women from seeking divorce by reducing already low AFDC benefits (Davidson, 1990).

Women are increasingly parenting alone because of demographic factors such as high female/male ratios in some areas and other societal changes. These families are much better off in cases where absentee fathers assume financial responsibility for raising their children. In the absence of such support, the rate of poverty among women and children is extremely high. Class and ethnic inequalities do limit the capacity of fathers to provide financial aid to their children. And fathers who are not able to or choose not to provide financial assistance to their children tend to be less involved in providing emotional, respite, and other task support that can enhance the quality of life for mother and child.

In Norway, the move toward an egalitarian society and improved standard of living for women is reflected in the Equal Status Act, which calls for increased opportunities for women to participate in the world of work and "equal distribution of responsibility, function and effort in the home" (Norwegian Research Council for Applied Social Sciences, 1988). This mandate can be applied to increased participation of absentee fathers in sharing parental responsibilities and also, perhaps, as a preventive measure to keep families together. Conflicts about child care and household responsibilities in the home are increasingly being recognized by family therapists as strong precursors to marital separation (McGoldrick et al., 1989).

The regulation of family functions in the "invisible area" of the home requires more ideological shifts rather than legislative mandates and policy initiatives. Nevertheless, the integration of coparental responsibilities into equality acts may serve to raise expectations in this regard and to facilitate the transition toward binuclear families, where absentee parents retain active roles in providing financial, emotional, and task support to their children.

REFERENCES

Adler, E. S., Bates, M., & Merdinger, J. M. (1985). Educational policies and programs for teenage parents and pregnant teenagers. *Family Relations, 34,* 183-187.

Ahron, C. R., & Rodgers, R. H. (1987). *Divorced families: Meeting the challenge of divorce and remarriage.* New York: W. W. Norton.

Ainsworth, L. L. (1984). Contact comfort: A consideration of the original work. *Psychological Reports, 55,* 943-949.

Allen, J., & Gordon, S. (1990). Creating a framework for change. In R. C. Meth & R. S. Pasick (Eds.), *Men in therapy: The challenge of change.* New York: Guilford.

Allen, J., & Laird, J. (1991). Men and story: constructing new narratives in therapy. In M. Bograd (Ed.), *Feminist approaches for men in family therapy.* New York: Haworth.

Amato, P. R. (1987). Family processes in one-parent, stepparent, and intact families: The child's point of view. *Journal of Marriage and the Family, 49,* 327-337.

Anderson, H., & Goolishian, H. (1988). Human systems as linguistic systems: Preliminary and evolving ideas about the implications for clinical theory. *Family Process, 27,* 371-393.

Arendell, T. (1986). *Mothers and divorce: Legal, economic and social dilemmas.* Berkeley: University of California Press.

Atteneave, C. (1980). Social networks as the unit of intervention. In P. Guerin (Ed.), *Family therapy.* New York: Gardner.

Avis, J. M. (1988). Deepening awareness: A private study guide to feminism and family therapy. In L. Braverman (Ed.), *Women, feminism, and family therapy.* New York: Haworth.

Azar, S., & Twentyman, C. (1986). Cognitive-behavioral perspectives on the assessment and treatment of child abuse. In *Advances in cognitive-behavioral research and therapy* (pp. 237-269). New York: Academic Press.

Bane, M. J., Ellwood, D. T., Jargowsky, P. H., & Wilson, J. B. (1989). *A research strategy on urban poverty.* Cambridge, MA: Harvard University, John F. Kennedy School of Government, Center for Health and Human Resources Policy.

Baumrind, D. (1980). New directions in socialization research. *American Psychologist, 35,* 739-752.

Beal, E. (1980). Separation, divorce, and single-parent families. In B. Carter & M. McGoldrick (Eds.), *The family life cycle: A framework for family therapy.* New York: Gardner.

Bell, W. M., Charping, J. W., & Strecker, J. B. (1988). Client perception of the effectiveness of divorce adjustment groups. *Journal of Social Service Research, 13*(2), 9-32.

Bloom, K. (1987, April 6). Raising a family: For women it pays to delay. *Business Week,* p. 26.

Bohorst, A., & Sirin, B. (1986). Women and the welfare state: A new form of political power. In H. Saasoon (Ed.), *Women and the welfare state.* London: Hutchinson.

Bowen, M. (1978). *Family therapy in clinical practice.* New York: Jason Aronson.

Boyd-Franklin, V. (1989). *Black families in therapy: A multisystem approach.* New York: Guilford.

Bricker-Jenkins, M., & Hooyman, N. (1986). *Not for women only: Social work practice for a feminist future.* Silver Springs, MD: National Association of Social Workers.

Brindis, C. D., & Jeremy, R. (1988). *Adolescent pregnancy and poverty in California: A strategic plan for action.* San Francisco: University of San Francisco.

Buchholz, E. S., & Gol, B. (1986). More than playing house: A developmental perspective on the strength in teenage motherhood. *American Journal of Orthopsychiatry, 56,* 347-359.

Burden, D. S., & Gottlieb, N. (1987). *The woman client: Providing human services in a changing world.* New York: Tavistock.

Caldwell, B., & Bradley, R. H. (1984). *Home observation for measurement of the environment* (rev. ed.). Little Rock: University of Arkansas Press.

Campbell, R. V., Lutzker, J. R., & Cuvo, A. J. (1982, May). *Comparative study of affection in low social economic families across status of abuse, neglect and non-abuse neglect.* Paper presented at the Eighth Annual Convention of the Association for Behavioral Analysis, Milwaukee, WI.

Caplan, J. J., & Hall-McCorquodale, I. (1985). Mother-blaming in major clinical journals. *American Journal of Orthopsychiatry, 55,* 345-353.

Cashion, B. G. (1982). Female-headed families: Effects on children and clinical implications. *Journal of Marital and Family Therapy, 8*(2), 77-86.

Cecchin, G. (1987). Hypothesizing, circularity and neutrality revisited: An invitation to curiosity. *Family Process, 26,* 405-413.

Cetron, M. J., Rocha, W., & Rebecca, L. (1988). Long term trends affecting the U.S. *Futurist, 1,* 29-40.

Chesler, P. (1986). *Mothers on trial: The battle for children and custody.* Seattle, WA: Seal.

Children's Defense Fund. (1986). *Adolescent pregnancy: What schools can do.* Washington, DC: Author.

Clingempeel, W. G., & Repucci, W. D. (1982). Joint custody after divorce. *Psychological Bulletin, 91,* 102-127.

Cobb, S. (1976). Social support as a moderator of life stress. *Psychosomatic Medicine, 38,* 301-314.

Colletta, N. D. (1983). At risk for depression: A study of young mothers. *Journal of Genetic Psychology, 142,* 301-310.

Collins, B. G. (1986). Defining feminist social work. *Social Work, 31,* 214-219.

Cramer, D. (1986). Gay parents and their children: A review of research and practical implications. *Journal of Counseling and Development, 64,* 504-507.

Crosbie, L., Burnett, M., & Newcomer, L. L. (1990). Children of divorce: The effects of multimodal intervention. *Journal of Divorce, 13*(3), 69-78.

Dahl, T. S. (1985). *Child welfare and social defence.* Oslo: Norwegian University Press.

Danziger, S. (1988). *The impact of federal policy change on working AFDC recipients.* Madison: University of Wisconsin, Institute for Research on Poverty.

Danziger, S. (1989). *Antipoverty policies and child poverty.* Ann Arbor: University of Michigan, School of Social Work.

Davidson, N. (1990). Life without father: America's greatest social catastrophe. *Policy Review, 51*(4), 40-44.

Davis, L. E., & Proctor, K. (1989). *Race, gender and class: Guidelines for practice with individuals, families and groups.* Englewood Cliffs, NJ: Prentice-Hall.

Devore, W., & Schlesinger, E. G. (1987). *Ethnic-sensitive social work practice* (2nd ed.). Columbus, OH: Charles E. Merrill.

DiLapi, E. M. (1989). Lesbian mothers and the motherhood hierarchy. *Journal of Homosexuality, 18*(1/2), 101-121.

Dornbusch, S. M., & Strober, M. H. (Eds.). (1988). *Feminism, children and the new families.* New York: Guilford.

Doudna, C. (1982, October 3). Weekend mother: Women without custody. *New York Times Magazine,* pp. 72-75.

Edelman, M. W. (1987). *Families in peril: An agenda for social change.* Cambridge, MA: Harvard University Press.

Edwards, D. J. A. (1984). The experience of interpersonal touch during a personal growth program: A factor analytic approach. *Human Relations, 37,* 769-780.

Elkind, D., & Bowen, R. (1979). Imaginary audience behavior in children and adolescents. *Developmental Psychologist, 15,* 38-44.

Epstein, A. (1980). *Assessing the child development information needed by adolescent parents with very young children.* Ypsilanti, MI: High/Scope Educational Research Foundation.

Erickson, G. (1975). The concept of personal network in clinical practice. *Family Process, 14,* 487-498.

Erickson, G. (1984). A framework and themes for social network interventions. *Family Process, 23,* 187-198.

Feldman, L. B. (1990). Fathers and fathering. In R. C. Meth & R. S. Pasick (Eds.), *Men in therapy: The challenge of change.* New York: Guilford.

Ferrier, M. J. (1986). Circular methods/indirect methods: The interview as an indirect technique. In S. de Shazer & R. Kral (Eds.), *Indirect approaches in therapy.* Rockville, MD: Aspen.

Figueira-McDonough, J., & Sarri, R. (Eds.). (1987). *The trapped woman: Catch-22 in deviance and control.* Newbury Park, CA: Sage.

Fisch, R., Weakland, J., & Segal, L. (1982). *The tactics of change: Doing therapy briefly.* San Francisco: Jossey-Bass.

Fox, F. M., & Hesse-Biber, S. (1984). *Women at work.* Palo Alto, CA: Mayfield.

Franklin, D. L. (1988). The impact of early childbearing on developmental outcomes: The case of black adolescent parenting. *Family Relations, 37,* 268-274.

Ganley, A. (1991). Feminist therapy with male clients. In M. Bograd (Ed.), *Feminist approaches for men in family therapy.* New York: Haworth.

148   SINGLE-PARENT FAMILIES

Garvin, C. D., & Seabury, B. (1984). *Interpersonal practice in social work: Processes and procedures*. Englewood Cliffs, NJ: Prentice-Hall.
Germain, C. B., & Gitterman, A. (1980). *The life model of social work practice*. New York: Columbia University Press.
Gilligan, C. (1982). *In a different voice: Psychological theory and women's development*. Cambridge, MA: Harvard University Press.
Gold, R. G., & Milner, J. S. (1983). Assessment of programs' effectiveness in selecting individuals "at risk" for problem parenting. *Journal of Clinical Psychology, 39*(3), 50-56.
Goldner, V. (1985). Warning: Family therapy may be dangerous to your health. *Family Therapy Networker, 9,* 19-23.
Goodrich, T. J., Rampage, C., & Ellman, B. (1989). The single mother. *Family Therapy Networker, 13,* 55-56.
Goodrich, T. J., Rampage, C., Ellman, B., & Halstead, K. (1988). *Feminist family therapy: A casebook*. New York: W. W. Norton.
Gordon, B. (1990a). Being a father. In R. C. Meth & R. S. Pasick (Eds.), *Men in therapy: The challenge of change* (pp. 247-260). New York: Guilford.
Gordon, B. (1990b). Men and fathers. In R. C. Meth & R. S. Pasick (Eds.), *Men in therapy: The challenge of change*. New York: Guilford.
Gottlieb, B. H. (1985). Combining lay and professional resources to promote human welfare: Prospects and tensions. In J. A. Yoder, J. N. L. Jonker, & R. H. B. Leaper (Eds.), *Support networks in a caring community*. Boston: Martinus Nijhoff.
Granger, J. M., & Portner, D. L. (1985). Ethnic and gender sensitive social work practice. *Journal of Social Work Education, 21,* 38-47.
Greif, G. L. (1985). *Single fathers*. Lexington, MA: Lexington.
Greif, G. L. (1987). Mothers without custody. *Social Work, 32,* 11-16.
Greif, G. L., & Pabst, M. (1988). *Mothers without custody*. Lexington, MA: Lexington.
Gunnarsdottir, H. E., & Broddason, P. (1984). *Kjor og Felagsleg Stada Einstaedra Foreldra*. Reykjavik, Iceland: Haskoli Islands, Felagsvisindadeild.
Hanmer, J., Stratham, D., & Sancier, B. (1989). *Women and social work: Toward a woman-centered practice*. Chicago: Lyceum.
Hanscombe, E., & Forster, J. (1981). *Rocking the cradle: Lesbian mothers, a challenge in family living*. Boston: Alyson.
Hartman, A. (1986, April). *Families in theory and practice*. Keynote address to the Second Annual Doctoral Symposium, Ohio State University College of Social Work.
Hartman, A., & Laird, J. (1983). *Family-centered social work practice*. New York: Free Press.
Hasenfeld, Y. (1987). Power in social work practice. *Social Service Review, 61,* 469-483.
Hatland, A. (1984). *The future of Norwegian social insurance*. Oslo: Institute of Applied Social Research.
Hawkins, W. E., & Duncan, D. F. (1985). Perpetrator of family characteristics related to child abuse and neglect: Comparison of substantiated and unsubstantiated reports. *Psychological Reports, 56,* 407-410.
Hernes, H. M. (1984). Women and the welfare state: The transition from private to public dependence. In H. Holter (Ed.), *Patriarchy in a welfare society* (pp. 26-45). Oslo: Norwegian University Press.
Hernes, H. M. (1987). *Welfare state and woman power*. Oslo: Norwegian University Press.
Hewlett, S. (1986). *A lesser life: The myth of women's liberation in America*. New York: William Morrow.

Hicks, S., & Anderson, C. (1989). Women on their own. In M. McGoldrick, C. Anderson, & F. Walsh (Eds.), *Women in families: A framework for family therapy.* New York: W. W. Norton.

Ho, M. K. (1987). *Family therapy with ethnic minorities.* Newbury Park, CA: Sage.

Hoffman, L. (1985). Beyond power and control: Toward a second order family systems therapy. *Family Systems Medicine, 3,* 381-396.

Hoffman, L. (1987). A co-evolutionary framework for systemic family therapy. In J. Hansen & B. Kenney (Eds.), *Diagnosis and assessment in family therapy.* Rockville, MD: Aspen.

Hopps, J. (1982). Oppression based on color. *Social Work, 27,* 51-55.

Hunger Action Forum. (1990, October). Vol. 3. (Published by the Hunger Project, Washington, DC)

Hunger Action Forum. (1991, February). Vol. 4. (Published by the Hunger Project, Washington, DC)

Imber-Black, E. (1986). Toward a resource model in systemic family therapy. In M. Karpel (Ed.), *Family resources: The hidden partner in family therapy.* New York: Guilford.

Imber-Black, E. (1988). *Families and larger systems: A family therapist's guide through the labyrinth.* New York: Guilford.

Kamerman, S. B., & Kahn, A. S. (1988). *Mothers alone: Strategies for a time of change.* Dover, MA: Auburn House.

Kamerman, S. B., & Kahn, A. S. (1989). The possibilities for child and family policy: A cross-national perspective. *Proceedings of the Academy of Political Science, 37*(2), 84-98.

Karpel, M. (Ed.). (1986). *Family resources: The hidden partner in family therapy.* New York: Guilford.

Keshet, H. F., & Rosenthal, K. M. (1988). Fathering after marital separation. *Social Work, 23,* 11-18.

King, U. (1989). *Women and spirituality: Voices of protest and promise.* London: Macmillan.

Kiresuk, T. J., & Lund, S. H. (1978). Goal attainment scaling. In C. C. Attkisson, W. A. Hargreaves, M. J. Horowitz, & J. E. Sorensen (Eds.), *Evaluation of new human service programs.* New York: Academic Press.

Kissman, K. (1991). Women caregivers, women wage earners: Social policy perspectives in Norway. *Women's Studies International Forum, 14,* 256-261.

Kissman, K. (1992). Parent skills training: Expanding school-based services for adolescent mothers. *Research on Social Work Practice, 2,* 161-171.

Kissman, K., & Shapiro, J. (1990). The composites of social support and well-being among adolescent mothers. *International Journal of Adolescents and Youth, 2,* 165-173.

Krausz, S. L. (1986). Sex roles within marriage. *Social Work, 31,* 457-464.

Leira, A. (1987). Time for work, time for care: Childcare in Norway. In J. Brannen & G. Wilson (Eds.), *Give and take in families: Studies in resource distribution.* Boston: Allen & Unwin.

Levy Simon, B. (1990). Rethinking empowerment. *Journal of Progressive Human Services, 1,* 27-39.

Lewis, E., & Kissman, K. (1989). Factors linking ethnic-sensitive and feminist social work practice with African-American women. *Arete, 14*(2), 23-31.

Lindblad-Goldberg, M. (Ed.). (1987). *Clinical issues in single-parent households.* Rockville, MD: Aspen.

Lowery, C. R., & Settle, S. A. (1985). Effects of divorce on children: Differential impact of custody and visitation patterns. *Family Relations, 34,* 455-464.

Lubeck, S., & Garrett, G. (1988). Child care 2000: Policy options for the future. *Social Policy, 18,* 31-37.

Lum, D. (1986). *Social work practice and people of color: A process-stage approach.* Monterey, CA: Brooks/Cole.

Lupenitz, D. A. (1988). *The family interpreted: Feminist theory in clinical practice.* New York: Basic Books.

Lutzker, J. R., Wesch, D., & Rice, J. M. (1984). A review of "Project 12-Ways": An ecobehavioral approach in the treatment and prevention of child abuse and neglect. *Advances in Behavioral Research and Therapy, 6,* 63-73.

Maluccio, A. N., & Marlow, W. D. (1974). The case for the contract. *Social Work, 19,* 28-36.

Masnick, G., & Bane, M. J. (1980). *The nation's families: 1960-1990.* Dover, MA: Auburn House.

McGoldrick, M. (1982). *Ethnic families.* New York: W. W. Norton.

McGoldrick, M., Anderson, C. M., & Walsh, F. (1989). *Women in families: A framework for family therapy.* New York: W. W. Norton.

McGuire, M., & Alexander, N. (1985). Artificial insemination of single women. *Fertility and Sterility, 43,* 182-184.

McLanahan, S. S. (1983). Family structure and stress: A longitudinal comparison of two-parent and female-headed families. *Journal of Marriage and the Family, 45,* 347-357.

Mendes, H. (1976). Single fatherhood. *Social Work, 21,* 308-312.

Meth, R. C., & Pasick, R. S. (Eds.). (1990). *Men in therapy: The challenge of change.* New York: Guilford.

Miller, S. (1986). *The good mother.* New York: Harper & Row.

Minifacts on equal rights. (1989). Oslo: Likestillingsradet (Equal Status Council).

Minuchin, S., & Fishman, C. (1981). *Family therapy techniques.* Cambridge, MA: Harvard University Press.

Moore, K. A. (1987). *Facts at a glance.* Washington, DC: Child Trends.

Morawetz, A., & Walker, G. (1984). *Brief therapy with single parent families.* New York: Brunner/Mazel.

Mulvey, L., & Vellenoweth, C. (1982). *Handbook for parent education for low-income families.* (Available from the authors, 3729 Tedrick Blvd., Fairfax, PA 22031)

Norwegian Research Council for Applied Social Sciences. (1988). *Research to promote equal status and gender equality: Programme memorandum.* Oslo: Author.

Orme, J. G., & Hamilton, M. A. (1987). Measuring knowledge of normative child development. *Social Service Review, 61,* 657-669.

O'Shea, M., & Phelps, R. (1985). Multiple family therapy: current status and critical appraisal. *Family Processes, 24,* 555-583.

Osherman, S. (1986). *Finding our fathers: The unfinished business of manhood.* New York: Free Press.

Pasick, R. (1990a). Friendship between men. In R. C. Meth & R. S. Pasick (Eds.), *Men in therapy: The challenge of change.* New York: Guilford.

Pasick, R. (1990b). Raised to work. In R. C. Meth & R. S. Pasick (Eds.), *Men in therapy: The challenge of change.* New York: Guilford.

Pasick, R., Gordon, S., &, Meth, R. (1990). Helping men understand themselves. In R. C. Meth & R. S. Pasick (Eds.), *Men in therapy: The challenge of change*. New York: Guilford.

Pasick, R., & White, C. (in press). Challenging General Patton: A feminist stance in substance abuse treatment and training. *Journal of Feminist Family Therapy*.

Paskowics, P. (1982). *Absentee mothers*. New York: Universal.

Pearce, D. (1990). Welfare is not for women: Why the war on poverty cannot conquer the feminization of poverty. In L. Gordon (Ed.), *Women, the state and welfare*. Madison: University of Wisconsin Press.

Penn, P. (1985). Feed-forward: Future questions, future maps. *Family Process, 24*, 299-310.

Pinderhughes, E. (1989). *Understanding race, ethnicity and power: The key to efficacy in clinical practice*. New York: Free Press.

Ponse, B. (1979). *Identities in the lesbian world: The social construction of self*. Westport, CT: Greenwood.

Quackenbush, R. L. (1987). Sex roles and social perception. *Human Relations, 40*, 659-670.

Radin, N., Oyserman, D., & Benn, R. (1991). Grandfathers, teen mothers and children under 2. In P. K. Smith (Ed.), *Psychology of grandparenthood*. London: Routledge.

Real, T. (1990). The therapeutic use of self in constructivist/systemic therapy. *Family Process, 29*, 255-272.

Richardson, L. (1986, February). Another world. *Psychology Today*, pp. 22-27.

Robinson, B., & Barret, R. (1986). *The developing father*. New York: Guilford.

Robitaille, J., Jones, E., Gold, R. G., Robertson, K. B., & Milner, J. (1985). Child abuse potentials and authoritarianism. *Journal of Clinical Psychology, 41*, 839-844.

Rohner, R. P. (1975). *They love me, they love me not: A worldwide study of the effects of parental acceptance and rejection*. New York: HRAF.

Roosa, M. W. (1986). Adolescent mothers, school drop-outs and school based intervention programs. *Family Relations, 35*, 313-317.

Rosenberg, M. S., & Repucci, N. D. (1985). Primary prevention of child abuse. *Journal of Consulting and Clinical Psychology, 52*, 576-585.

Rothblum, E., & Franks, V. (1987). Custom-fitted straitjackets: Perspectives on women's mental health. In J. Figueira-McDonough & R. Sarri (Eds.), *The trapped woman: Catch-22 in deviance and control*. Newbury Park, CA: Sage.

Sands, R. G., & Muccio, K. E. (1989). Mother-headed single parent families: A feminist perspective. *Affilia, 4*(3), 25-41.

Sanford, L. T., & Donovan, M. E. (1989). *Women and self-esteem: Understanding the way we think and feel about ourselves*. London: Penguin.

Sarason, I. G., & Sarason, B. R. (1982). Concomitants of social support: Attitudes, personality characteristics and life experiences. *Journal of Personality, 50*, 331-445.

Segal, M. (1985). A study of maternal beliefs and values within the context of an intervention program. In I. Sigel (Ed.), *Parental belief systems: The psychosocial consequences for children*. Hillsdale, NJ: Lawrence Erlbaum.

Selvini-Pallazoli, M., Boscolo, L., Cecchin, G., & Prata, G. (1980). Hypothesizing, circularity, neutrality: Three guidelines for the conductor of the session. *Family Processes, 19*, 2-12.

Shore, B. (1986, May 28-31). *NASW preliminary report: Single heads of household.* Paper presented at the National Association of Social Workers National Conference on Women's Issues, Atlanta, GA.

Stier, D. S., & Hall, J. A. (1984). Gender differences in touch: An empirical theoretical review. *Journal of Personality and Social Psychology, 47,* 440-459.

Surrey, J. L. (1985). *Self-in-relations: A theory of women's development.* Working Paper, Wellesley College, Stone Center for Developmental Services and Studies.

Takas, M. (1987). *Child custody: A complete guide for concerned mothers.* New York: Harper & Row.

Tereszkiewics, L. (1984). Survey documents: Problems of pregnant and parenting teens. *Youth Law News, 8*(3), 17-19.

Thompson, M. S. (1986). The influence of supportive relations on the psychological well-being of teenage mothers. *Social Forces, 64,* 1006-1024.

Tomm, K. (1988). Interventive interviewing: Part III. Intending to ask circular, strategic, or reflexive questions? *Family Process, 27,* 1-16.

Tracy, E. M. (1990). Identifying social support resources of at risk families. *Social Work, 35*(3), 29-34.

U.S. Bureau of the Census. (1985). *Money, income and poverty status of families in the U.S.: 1984.* Washington, DC: Government Printing Office.

U.S. Bureau of the Census. (1989a). *Marital status and living arrangement: March, 1988* (Current Population Reports, Series P-20, No. 433). Washington, DC: Government Printing Office.

U.S. Bureau of the Census. (1989b). *Money, income and poverty status of families and persons in the United States: 1988* (Series P-60, No. 165). Washington, DC: Government Printing Office.

Van Den Bergh, N., & Cooper, L. B. (Eds.). (1986). *Feminist visions for social work.* Silver Springs, MD: National Association of Social Workers.

Vukelich, C., & Klerman, D. S. (1985). Mature and teenage mothers. *Family Relations, 34,* 189-196.

Wallerstein, J. C. (1986). Women after divorce: Preliminary report from a ten-year follow-up. *American Journal of Orthopsychiatry, 56,* 65-77.

Walters, M. (1988). Single-parent, female-headed households. In M. Walters, B. Carter, P. Papp, & O. Silverstein (Eds.), *The invisible web: Gender patterns in family relationships.* New York: Free Press.

Walters, M., Carter, B., Papp, P., & Silverstein, O. (Eds.). (1980). *The invisible web: Gender patterns in family relationships.* New York: Free Press.

Weinberg, M. S., Swensson, R. G., & Hammersmith, S. K. (1983). Sexual autonomy and the status of women: Models of female sexuality in U.S. sex manuals from 1950 to 1980. *Social Problems, 30,* 312-324.

Weitzman, L. J. (1985). *The divorce revolution: The unexpected social and economic consequences for women and children in America.* New York: Free Press.

Weitzman, L. J., Baters, C., Chesler, P., & Munger, D. (1986, February). Beneath the surface: The truth about divorce, custody and support. *Ms.,* pp. 67-70.

West, G. (1981). *The national welfare rights movement: The social protest of poor women.* New York: Praeger.

White, M., & Epston, D. (1990). *Narrative means to therapeutic ends.* New York: W. W. Norton.

Whittaker, J. K., & Tracy, E. M. (1989). *Social treatment: An introduction to interpersonal helping in social work practice* (2nd ed.). Hawthorne, NY: Aldine de Gruyter.

Wise, S., & Grossman, F. K. (1980). Adolescent mothers and their infants: Psychological factors in early attachment and interaction. *American Journal of Orthopsychiatry, 50,* 454-468.

Index

ABOUT THE AUTHORS

KRIS KISSMAN is an Assistant Professor at the University of Michigan School of Social Work. She has published a number of articles related to the welfare of mother-headed families, noncustodial parenting, and adolescent mothers. Her research interests include gender-sensitive interventions and social policies and programs that strengthen impoverished families. Ethnicity- and class-sensitive social work practice with diverse families is an integral part of her work. Her recent publications and work in progress are focused on cross-national analyses of the welfare of mothers and children in Scandinavia, the United States, and Latin America.

JO ANN ALLEN was a faculty member of the University of Michigan School of Social Work for more than 20 years and is now Professor Emeritus. She taught family theory and family-centered social work practice and has a number of publications in family therapy books and journals. She maintains an active clinical practice, working with individuals, couples, and single-parent families. She offers continuing education for family therapists through an affiliation with the Ann Arbor Center for Family Research and Training. She also serves as a consultant to several agencies and conducts workshops at local, state, and national levels. One of her major interests in recent years has concerned gender issues in clinical practice. Her most recent publication in that area is the chapter she contributed to *Men in Therapy: The Challenge of Change,* edited by Richard Meth and Robert Pasick.